THE *Queen's Counsel* OFFICIAL LAWYERS' HANDBOOK

THE *Queen's Counsel* OFFICIAL LAWYERS' HANDBOOK

DANIEL R. WHITE AND ALEX WILLIAMS

The Robson Press

First published in Great Britain in 2011 by
The Robson Press
Biteback Publishing Ltd
Westminster Tower
3 Albert Embankment
London
SE1 7SP

Some of the material in this book previously appeared in *The Official Lawyer's Handbook* by Daniel R. White, published in 1991.

ISBN 978-1-84954-170-1

10 9 8 7 6 5 4 3 2 1

A CIP catalogue record for this book is available from the British Library.

Set in Flatform and Dolly by Namkwan Cho
Printed and bound in Great Britain by TJ International, Padstow, Cornwall

CONTENTS

Foreword by Tim Kevan ix

Introduction 1
20 Good Reasons to Become a Lawyer — *13 Hard Facts about Lawyers*

1. Determining Your Legal Aptitude 9
14 Questions Revealing Your Suitability for the Profession

2. Getting onto a Law Degree Course 17
Reading Comprehension — *Analytical Reasoning* — *Evaluation of Facts*

3. Passing Your Law Degree 23
The Socractic Method — *Law Students and Law Tutors* — *The Graduate Diploma in Law (GDL) in a Nutshell (Contracts, Civil Procedure, Torts, Real Property)*

4. Summer Placements 53

5. Legal Practice Course (LPC) 57
Coping with Fear: Continue to Write — *14 Practical Skills They Ought to Teach You in Law School - But Don't*

6. Recruiting 65
The On-Campus Screening — *The Formal Interview* — *Recruiting Lunches* — *Your Curriculum Vitae* — *The Covering Letter* — *Photos*

— *Recruiting Letters: What Do They Really Mean?* — *Recruiting Misrepresentations* — *Hard Questions*

7. How to Survive (and Make Partner) in Your Law Firm 87
Rule 1: Cover Your Arse — *Rule 2: Take on as few Files as Possible* — *Rule 3: There is No Such Thing as a 'Draft'* — *Rule 4: Cultivate the Image of a Workhorse* — *Rule 5: Avoid Peripheral Involvement in Anything* — *Rule 6: Give Partners What they Want* — *Rule 7: Stay Alert to Your Long-Term Prospects*

8. Once You're a Partner 133
The Small Firm — *Types of Lawyer* — *The Big Firm*

9. Elements of Style: The Lawyerly Look 143
The Men — *The Women* — *The Briefcase*

10. The Bar 149
Choosing an Inn — *Pupillage* — *Getting a Pupillage* — *The Clerks* — *Getting a Tenancy* — *Being a Barrister* — *Advocacy*

11. Alternative Legal Careers 157
Civil Service — *Country Practice*

12. Legal Writing 161
'Speaking as a Lawyer...' — *'The Sky is Blue'* — *10 Principles of Legal Writing*

13. Drafting Legal Documents 167
Types of Legal Documents — *How to Draft a Contract from Scratch* — *Drafting and Punctuation: The Perils of Full Stops* — *Among v. Between* — *Legal Machismo* — *The Myth of the Reasonable Contract*

14. Women in the Law 175
The Crusader — *The Mata Hari* — *The Survivor*

15. Lawyers and Humour 181
Legal Graffiti

16. The Courts 183
Litigation Posturing: Indignation, Moral Outrage and Four Other Essential Poses — 10 Commandments of Courtroom Conduct

17. Legal Ethics and Other Great Oxymorons 191
How Far Can You Go? — Courtesy Among lawyers

18. The Creative Art of Billing 195
Double-Billing — What the Time-Sheet Says & What the Time-Sheet Should Say

19. Lawyers in Love 201
6 Things to Bring with You on Your First Date with a Lawyer — Spotting (and Avoiding) Lawyers Out on the Town

20. You and Your Lawyer 211
Selecting Your Lawyer — You Call the Tune — Doctors v. Lawyers

21. Beyond Law 219
Top 10 Things You Can Do With Your Law Degree Other Than Practise Law

22. Legal Glossary 223

FOREWORD

There's something about the law that invites satire. There's the body of the law itself, an ever-growing bunch of rules and regulations which nits and picks its way into all of our lives on a daily basis. Then there are the various institutions set up ostensibly to increase respect for the processes, such as swanning around in eighteenth-century horsehair wigs and gowns and dining out in medieval halls. But above all, it's the characters within the profession that provide such scope for humour. A huge collection of often extremely able and articulate individuals suddenly taking on the demeanour of 'the lawyer' – the various turns of phrase that start to slip out, the formal ways of drafting documents and then the way they talk to each other in court. That's before you start looking at the various disputes that can arise, the clients who bring them and not forgetting the all-important judges.

It's against this theatrical backdrop that Daniel R. White and Alex Williams bring this wonderful updated version of the Official Lawyers' Handbook. It's an exciting collaboration that brings together two of the very best legal satirists around. Daniel is the author of numerous books of legal comedy and Alex has been penning his hilarious Queen's Counsel cartoons for *The Times* and for his associated books for many years, as well as illustrating my own BabyBarista characters for *The Guardian*. They follow very clearly in the tradition of the great legal satirists of the past such as A. P. Herbert and his *Uncommon Law*, Theo Mathew's *Forensic Fables* and A. Laurence Polak's *Legal*

Fictions, and it's not an over-statement to say that they do that tradition more than justice.

Yet the wonderful irony of the book is that despite the fact that it explicitly sets out to caricature and tease the profession, something which would entertain lawyers and non-lawyers alike, it is also an excellent guide for those thinking of entering what in my opinion remains a wonderful profession in which to practise. Not just because it gives them a taste of the dark humour that provides so much of the entertainment and enjoyment for lawyers in the course of their work but also because it may even provide a few useful insights into the realities of day-to-day life in the law, albeit indirectly. With all of this in mind, it is a privilege to introduce this book.

Tim Kevan
Author of the BabyBarista novels *Law and Peace* and *Law and Disorder* (both published by Bloomsbury).

INTRODUCTION

The Great Recession, depression, credit crunch, temporary blip – however you want to refer to the current state of the economy – the verdict is now in: the legal profession has been hard hit by it too, almost as if it were an ordinary part of the British economy. As if law were actually a ... *business*.

Gone are the days when 'growth', 'bonus' and 'Beijing office' were the words most frequently intoned across the mahogany tables of panelled conference rooms in Broadgate offices. Recent bywords have been 'caution', 'budget' and 'If we don't get rid of twenty bodies by Christmas I'll be earning less than twice what some of my clients earn'.

We have all seen the signs of this leaner, meaner era – families losing their homes, pensioners losing their life savings and ordinary people losing their jobs by the million. But can any of these compare to the heart-rending sight of a lawyer losing his Aston Martin?

Some things are just too painful to contemplate.

Hence the rush of benevolent folk to donate food, clothing, even the second family car to the nearest suffering lawyer.

Not that all sectors of the law bore the brunt equally. Insolvency lawyers have never had it so good. As company after company went down the tubes, carrying investors, employees and years of experience with it, the lawyers who specialise in corporate euthanasia prospered. They spent profitable hours scavenging corporate battlefields, firing bullets of mercy into the heads of expiring conglomerates, over-geared property companies and the beleaguered remains of the credit crunch and the banking crisis. Dirty work indeed, but then *life* is dirty.

Feeling the squeeze more than any other group are the law students. Law firms are still sending teams to university recruitment fairs but, because clients have been feeling the pinch – which means law firms feeling the pinch – the demand for trainee solicitors or for baby barristers who know fresh air about anything useful plummeted. All this meant, and continues to mean, fewer vacancies and more competition among students. And, for those lucky enough to score a training contract, many have been deferred a year by their future firms, waiting for an economic upturn.

It's not even as if those who got in when times were better are enjoying complete security. The profligate recruiting policies of the boom years have come home to roost, with a flood of people qualifying into a profession with many fewer vacancies.

At one big City firm, associates told to take a walk used to be given a six-month grace period to find another job. Now the grace period has dropped to three months, and the word on the street is that it's coming down to an hour and a half.

In recent years, average associate salaries have done the unthinkable: after a decade of regular sizeable increases, they have stalled. Ok, they're not actually falling, but that isn't good news when your salary is the one thing that makes it worthwhile getting out of bed in the morning. That is if you've got a bed to get out of.

There is no safety now even for partners, traditionally as immune from quality and productivity requirements as the Royal Family. Unproductive partners are being eased out or unceremoniously dumped, as if they were ... *associates*. And because of what? Mere *dispensability*. How the mighty are fallen.

Some argue that the only people getting the boot are those whose firms were already looking for an excuse to get rid of them – in effect, deadwood. Maybe, but consider the implications: if you weed out the slowest five runners in a ten person race, the average pace goes up for everyone. Law firms are speeding up, going faster and harder than ever, and it's going to be that way for the foreseeable future.

A kinder and gentler profession? Hardly. A thousand points of light? More like a thousand pints of blood.

So what, you ask?

For most people, news about starving lawyers carries its own justification. It's inherently pleasing. But if you're a lawyer yourself, in the process of becoming one, or even just thinking about it, the 'so what' is that the competition in the legal profession is more vicious than ever. You need all the help you can get.

You need this book!

The Queen's Counsel Official Lawyer's Handbook walks you through every step of your legal career, from pre-exam bowel-liquification to the holy grail of partnership. Starting with that make-or-break first year of your law degree, it provides enough key concepts and buzzwords to put you at the top of your class – as well as into bed with at least two of your fellow students by the Christmas holidays.

But this book is more than just a ticket to success in university and law school. It's an *alternative* to both of them, offering better preparation for a legal career than anything you'll get at the College of Law. It offers not only obscure jargon and archaic concepts, but sufficient training in the art of hair-splitting and issue-obfuscation to enable you to alienate complete strangers in the space of just minutes – a skill that some lawyers don't acquire for weeks.

All this for less than the price of dinner at Pizza Express!

20 GOOD REASONS TO BECOME A LAWYER
(Why not? Everyone else is!)

1. The money.
2. You've got a degree in history, which just about qualifies you to sell suits at Hackett.
3. You think people who carry oversized black briefcases have an aura of worldly power.
4. Your Uncle Fred is a lawyer.

5. The money.

6. You're a genius, you know it, and you think becoming a lawyer is the best way to make sure everyone else knows it.

7. Your parents don't want to break a seven-generation succession of lawyers going back to your great-great-great-great-grandfather Bert, who migrated to London from Llanwelwyn with his wife Gwyneth and half a sack of coal.

8. You want to change the world.

9. You want to own the world.

10. You're going thin on top and you think wearing a wig at the Bar is a better bet than a Wayne Rooney transplant.

11. You want to get out of doing jury service.

12. The money.

13. When you were twelve you spent your entire life savings on a train set that broke down in two hours, since when your sole purpose in living has been to sue the swine who sold it to you and reduce him to servile beggary.

14. The money.

15. You were president of your university debating team and always loved the panic-struck look on the face of your opponent as you took his argument to pieces.

16. You think most male lawyers look like Tom Cruise.

17. You think most female lawyers look like Rachel Weisz.

18. You're Jewish and don't want to be a doctor.

19. You want to teach law because it's common knowledge that law tutors have lots of affairs with their students.

20. The money.

If you're already out of law school, this book is even more critical. It shows you how to get into one of those prestigious, high-paying, hand-stitched-shoe law firms and, more difficult, how to survive once you're there.

You didn't go to law school so you could spend the next five years working in a call centre. You've already done all that. You're ready now for the status that comes from doing something truly unproductive, parasitic and mercenary. You're ready now to be a … a … LAWYER.

And not just any kind of lawyer. Not for you a two-room office above Tesco Metro in Peckham High Street. You want to be a legal honcho – an adviser to politicians, bank presidents and other big-time criminals. You want a plush corner office, embossed stationery, a calfskin briefcase and a secretary who has the organisational skills of a supercomputer. But with nicer legs.

13 HARD FACTS ABOUT LAWYERS
(Do you realise what they actually do for a living?)

1.   The average lawyer earns less per hour than a plumber.

2.   The odds are that you personally will not do better than the average lawyer.

3.   Everyone you know despises lawyers.

4.   The thought of spending 80 per cent of the rest of your waking life behind a desk in an office in Moorgate makes you want to throw up.

5.   Recent research has shown that 78 per cent of practising lawyers are wider at the stomach than the shoulders.

6.   People charged with murder and rape – your likely clients if you practise criminal law – are usually guilty as sin.

7.   The number of law graduates who get jobs at the top-earning firms is about the same as the number who become jackaroos on Australian sheep farms, and the latter are happier.

8.   Saddam Hussein used to be thought of as a nice guy before he attended law school.

9.   A 'light' day in a large law firm runs from 8 a.m. to 8 p.m.

10.   A 'light' week consists of six and a half light days.

11.   Most male lawyers look more like John Mortimer than Tom Cruise.

12.   So do most female lawyers.

13.   Studies show that the average law tutor has only 7.3 sexual encounters with law students per year.

This book tells you how to get them.

It's not just for lawyers, though. It is also essential reading for 'lay people' (what lawyers call the people they screw). Which of us has not at one time or another said, 'I'm going to sue the bastard if it's the last thing I do!'? The rub is, only a lawyer knows *how* to sue the bastard. If you, a lay person, want to start an action, you have to instruct a lawyer, which, like hiring a member of an even older profession, may be easy but it's not cheap.

The legal profession is too important to remain veiled in secrecy. It pervades our existence. Whether you want to start a business, buy a house or sue the doctor who assured you that the sex change operation was reversible – you need to know the law. To your utter distaste, you'll have to deal with a lawyer.

But you don't have to be at your lawyer's mercy simply because up to now you've never understood what he was up to.

Read this book, and you'll know where your lawyer is coming from, how he got there, and just where 'there' is.

You'll know what lawyers do – and how to stop them doing it to you.

CHAPTER 1

DETERMINING YOUR LEGAL APTITUDE

*Tunnel-visioned workaholic ...
or double-visioned alcoholic?*

Not everyone is cut out for a legal career. So before commencing the training in this book, take the following self-assessment test to find out whether you have what it takes to be a lawyer, or whether you would be better employed in a productive sector of the economy. You might discover that you really aren't suited to it at all. Better to find out now, before your vocabulary becomes permanently encrusted with Latin. You might also discover, if your score is high, that you aren't suited to anything *else* – in which case this book will prove to have been the best investment of your life. (For answers and a grading scale, see page 16.)

1. When you wake up each day, the first thing you do is:
    (a) Hit the snooze control.

(b) Turn on the afternoon news to see what you missed that morning.

(c) Try to ascertain the age, gender and species of whatever is sleeping beside you – without waking it up.

(d) Make the bed, polish your shoes to a gloss, write a letter to mother and recite the *White Book* – all before breakfast.

2. If a partner told you to spend the next two weeks proofreading the *White Book*, you would:

(a) Lose your lunch on the spot.

(b) Say that, as flattered as you are to receive such an important job, Anderson down the hall told you only yesterday that he dreams of such work and, well, who are you to stand in the way of a colleague's dreams?

(c) Accept the assignment cheerfully – and then email your stockbroker to short as many shares of Thomson Reuters PLC as he can lay his hands on.

(d) Say you don't see any reason you couldn't complete the job by next Monday.

3. When you were a child, you experienced lust in the presence of

(a) Your parent of the opposite sex.

(b) Either parent's briefcase.

(c) Your Great Dane, Chewy.

(d) Shakespeare's Great Dane, Hamlet.

4. Word Association: when you hear the word 'prison', the first thing that comes to your mind is:

(a) Unsafe sex.

(b) Boarding school.

(c) Your last income tax return.

(d) Establishing an alibi.

(e) All of the above – in that order.

5. At the end of *Harry Potter and the Deathly Hallows, Part 1,* you were left with:
   (a) A feeling of uneasiness at watching the tribulations of a young wizard and his loyal friends on the run from their enemies.
   (b) A feeling of uneasiness at having chosen *Harry Potter* over *Transformers 2.*
   (c) A feeling of emptiness from watching a two and a half hour film without an ending on a single packet of popcorn.
   (d) A feeling of numbness in your bum from sitting through any film that lasts over two hours.

6. Your favourite colour is:
   (a) Pea green.
   (b) Conference-table brown.
   (c) Ash grey – your face in the mirror after seven all-nighters before Finals.
   (d) Blue – preferably the exact shade of counsel's notebooks.

7. Word Association: when you hear the word 'security', the first thing that comes to your mind is:
   (a) The stuffed bear you still kiss and whisper 'Goodnight' to every night.
   (b) The 72-function Swiss Army knife you carry in your pocket whenever you visit friends south of the river.
   (c) Negligence insurance.
   (d) A comfort letter from Linklaters.

8. If you were to drive over a dog that had darted into the street, your first impulse would be to:
   (a) Feel concern that it might be alive and suffering.
   (b) Roll up your window. I mean, good God, it's hard enough to talk to Hong Kong on one's mobile without that infernal howling in the background. You'd think the beast was

dying... Well okay, but that's still no excuse for such a horrific sound. We all have our troubles, don't you see? I personally wouldn't make a sound like that if it was the last thing I ever... That is, if he'd just quiet down a bit he could expire at his leisure, and perhaps get a bit of sympathy, rather than have every man, woman and child within twenty miles urging him to get on with it, for God's sake.

(c) Try to find the owner to demand payment for the dent in your car.

(d) Reverse over it again to teach it a lesson.

9. When you think of lawyers, you envision people who:
   (a) Protect the downtrodden.
   (b) Exploit the proletariat.
   (c) Couldn't get a job in productive sectors of the economy.
   (d) You try not to think about lawyers.

10. Which of the following do you consider most likely to guarantee success in the law?
    (a) A precise, analytical mind.
    (b) The ability to lie like a politician.
    (c) A level Latin.
    (d) This book.

11. If a sexual opportunity presented itself right now, you would:
    (a) Go for it, no matter where you are, who you are with, or what it might do to the rest of your life.
    (b) Ascertain whether he/she has some form of contraception, has anything that looks like a cold sore, or shows more than a passing interest in the plot of *Single White Female*.
    (c) Call all your friends to let them know it's finally about to happen.
    (d) Be too stunned to act.

12. During your idle moments, you fantasise about:
    (a) Winning a class action against BP.
    (b) Oral arguments before the Court of Appeal.
    (c) Oral acts with the models in the Agent Provocateur catalogue.
    (d) Joining a City firm so you wouldn't have to worry about any more idle moments.

13. The first thing that comes into your mind when you look at the ink blot below is:

    (a) The Jackson Pollock in your firm's conference room.
    (b) A hit-and-run victim (and potential client).
    (c) The insanity defence.
    (d) Prefer to research the issue before commenting.

14. Your idea of a great time is:
    (a) A late night at the office proofreading loan agreements.
    (b) Around-the-clock negotiations on a corporate takeover.
    (c) Foreclosing a mortgage on a widow with six young, handicapped children.
    (d) Nothing remotely resembling any of the above.

NOW CHECK YOUR SCORE

Points Tally
1. (a) 0   (b) 1   (c) 2   (d) 7

2. (a) 0   (b) 1   (c) 7   (d) 2
3. (a) 1   (b) 1   (c) 6   (d) 2
4. (a) 5   (b) 3   (c) 2   (d) 6
5. (a) 0   (b) 4   (c) 5   (d) 6
6. (a) 0   (b) 4   (c) 4   (d) 7
7. (a) 0   (b) 2   (c) 2   (d) 7
8. (a) 0   (b) 0   (c) 5   (d) 7
9. (a) 2   (b) 5   (c) 0   (d) 0
10. (a) 0   (b) 5   (c) 4   (d) 7
11. (a) 1   (b) 5   (c) 3   (d) 1
12. (a) 5   (b) 7   (c) 1   (d) 7
13. (a) 1   (b) 5   (c) 5   (d) 7
14. (a) 7   (b) 6   (c) 7   (d) 0

If you scored:

65–93
Congratulations – sort of. You're compulsive, calculating, avaricious and sexually repressed. You could make it to the very top of the legal profession.

45–64
Not bad. You have the makings of a lawyer, maybe even partnership material. Sometimes you let your feelings for humanity interfere with your professional role, but with work you could learn to repress those feelings.

20–44
Ok, so you're not going to be the youngest partner in your firm's history. So what? You're a likeable person with a bright life ahead of you. Enjoy!

0–20
You've gone too far the other way. You're a weak-kneed, hand-wringing jellyfish without an ounce of gumption. Pull yourself

together and try to make something of your life – but not in
the law.

CHAPTER 2

GETTING ONTO A LAW DEGREE COURSE

Square pegs in square holes

University law departments aren't interested in the 'whole person', quirks and all. They don't want to hear about anyone's individuality, except for purposes of quashing it. Their objective, frankly stated, is to pick applicants as similar as possible and then, over the next three years, render them more so. They want uniformity, and to get it they're prepared to hone, sand and polish away any distinguishing characteristics, so that you and your classmates will match each other as perfectly as, well, as a set of third-year law graduates.

You swam the Channel in ski boots? So what? You can play the harp with your feet? So what? You ran your school's chess club and were the first male in the school's history to play Lady Macbeth? Again – so what? There are three things law school admissions officers don't do about those things, and all three of them are care. Law schools need more wacky non-conformists like the *Titanic* needed more on-board ice trays.

Law departments look at one thing and one thing only: your exam results. They just plug the figures into a formula and take as many applicants as they have room for, discounted by the number of people who will die, go to other schools, or decide there must be a less painful way to gird one's loins for life.

What about all those requests for character references? Why must you produce written evidence that you wouldn't touch a choirboy with a ten-foot priest?

These are tools for *weeding people out*, not bringing them in. The admissions people are hoping to learn something that will justify kicking you out of contention, thus sparing them from reading one more application.

So the applications don't really matter? If you got the right scores on your entrance exam, your application form could show you to be barely literate (notwithstanding your doctoral thesis, 'Best Begging Pitches on the London Underground') and you'd still get in. Your references could say nothing but that your methadone treatment appears to be working, and you'd still get in.

The good news is that there are plenty of spaces to go round. Over seventy colleges and universities that offer law degrees do not require you to take the CPE (Certificate of Proficiency in English). Thus, pretty much any ambulatory primate can get in *somewhere*.

But it's getting tougher. One of the consequences of the recent banking crisis is that today's young-and-greedy are returning to the law in droves. Numbers have also risen due to films and television, which have glamorised the profession, giving it a kind of highbrow chic. This is ironic, since they depict law practice about as accurately as the pages of *Hello* depict marriage.

The bad news is that the NQ prospects (that's *newly qualified* to you) at the other end are looking dicier and dicier, with fewer training contracts expected for 2012. That's why it's important to get onto a law course that the law firms have heard of (remember you'll be interviewing for a trainee position in your final year). The only sure way of doing that is to go hell for leather for those exam results. There may well be some well-rounded likeable people in the top firms, but that isn't what got them there. Straight As are what you need.

So ... have you got what it takes to make it in the law? Is your mind a steel trap or a lump of tofu? Take the following test, which was carefully designed by trained auto mechanics to help you find out.

READING COMPREHENSION

1. *'It was the best of times, it was the worst of times, it was the age of wisdom, it was the age of foolishness ... it is a far, far better rest that I go to than I have ever known.'*

Question: In the above novel, what time is it?
   (a) The best of times
   (b) The worst of times
   (c) The *Sunday Times*
   (d) About two o'clock

2. *'Know thyself.'*

Question: In the above passage, the writer is:
   (a) Plagiarising Plato.
   (b) Employing an archaic usage.
   (c) Advocating a solipsistic approach to epistemology.
   (d) Describing your social life.

ANALYTICAL REASONING

1. *Einstein's theory of relativity postulated that there can be no motion at a speed greater than that of light in a vacuum, and time is dependent on the relative motion of an observer measuring the time. If a hydrogen atom electron is accelerated at a rate of π / speed of light through an inverse*

hyper magnetic positron field and then bombarded with neutrons from a nuclear haemorrhoidal pile in a critical core reaction, what time is it?

   (a) The best of times.

   (b) The worst of times.

   (c) Time to think about business school.

   (d) About two o'clock.

2. *For a dinner party, Sophie must prepare several different three-bean salads, using chilli beans, lentil beans, lima beans, kidney beans, soya beans and has beans. Unfortunately,*

   (i) *lima beans and lentils do not taste good together, and*

   (ii) *kidney beans and soya beans do not look good together, and*

   (iii) *chilli beans and garbanzos render human beings incapable of holding solid food.*

Within these restrictions, identify which of the indicated number of bean combinations satisfy the following criteria:

   (a) Two salads that resemble the bottom of a bird cage.

   (b) Four stews that would have her dinner guests exchanging embarrassed glances after a single mouthful.

   (c) Three ratatouilles that would lead a goat to check the bottoms of its hooves.

   (d) None of the above. If you want to be a bean counter, take your accountancy exams.

3. *Ramona said 'All dogs bark. This animal does not bark. Therefore this animal is not a dog.'*

Which of the following most closely parallels the logic of the foregoing syllogism?

   (a) Cats do not bark. Cats climb trees. Trees have bark.

   (b) Lawyers overcharge. Taxi meters overcharge. Lawyers are taxi meters.

   (c) George sells cars. Every car sold by George falls apart. George is a used Rover dealer.

(d) Dogs bay at the moon. Your girlfriends bay at the moon. You would be better off getting to know thyself.

EVALUATION OF FACTS

1. Murder consists of (i) the death of a human being, and (ii) an intent to cause death or grievous bodily harm. Apply these rules to the following factual situation:

Ronnie, a London scrap metal dealer, enters Jean-Paul's Unisex Barbershop in a tough section of town. While he is waiting for a trim, an employee of Jean-Paul's sees him and, mistaking him for somebody else, runs a chain saw through the upper half of his head.

Question: On trial for murder, the employee should be found:

(a) Guilty of taking too much off the top.

(b) Not guilty because of assumption-of-risk principles regarding unisex barbershops.

(c) Guilty, but nevertheless qualified for the Metropolitan Police Force.

(d) About two o'clock.

CHAPTER 3

PASSING YOUR LAW DEGREE

Are you telling me Socrates did it this way?

Legal lore recognises three distinct periods in the standard three-year degree:

In the first year, they *scare* you to death.
In the second, they *work* you to death.
In the third, they *bore* you to death.

The most memorable aspect of the first year – fear – follows from having to learn a host of completely alien concepts, e.g. getting up for a 9 a.m. lecture. It also results from exposure to the Socratic method of teaching, more commonly referred to as 'learning through humiliation'. (More on this later.)

In your second year, fear gives way to a period of frenetic overwork brought on by insecurity. Based on first-year grades, only 10 per cent of the class now ranks in the top 10 per cent of the class – a phenomenon that the more reflective among you might have anticipated. But 100 per cent of the class *is used* to ranking in the top 10 per cent. Those who now make up the bottom 90 per cent feel confused and anxious – even desperate. Consistent with the modus operandi that got them into law school in the first place, they channel their anxiety into hard work.

As for the boredom in the third year, you would have noticed this in the first year if you hadn't been so scared.

The Socratic Method

The Socratic method of teaching, which first became fashionable in the USA, has gained popularity in the more civilised regions of the English-speaking world. Its goal is to improve on the typical classroom situation in which a professor reads a prepared lecture to his students at a nice even pace, and they in turn show their respect by writing down everything he says – word for word. The one problem in this otherwise efficient transfer of information is that it is accomplished without troubling anyone's brain. (Actually, that may be its chief virtue. We'll have to study that and get back to you.)

By way of contrast with such ritualistic note-taking, the Socratic method involves a dialogue between the professor and a chosen student, with the student pressed to answer ever more complex levels of questioning about a given case or issue.

Not unlike the philosopher after whom it was named, the Socratic method was, and remains, controversial. On the one hand, its potential pedagogic value indisputably surpasses that of the old-fashioned lecture, which causes an extraordinary number of what physicians call 'false positives' for narcolepsy. On the other hand, few of even the most devoted apostles of the Socratic method have proven adept at its use.

First, few professors are willing to jettison all those yellowing lecture notes they've spent so many years compiling, and even fewer are capable of replacing those notes with effective Socratic instruction.

Innumerable class hours are wasted in the following way:

TUTOR SMITH: Ms Ellis, are you with us today?

STUDENT ELLIS: Yes.

TUTOR SMITH: Then let us proceed. What am I thinking?

STUDENT ELLIS: I beg your pardon?

TUTOR SMITH: What thought is passing through my mind at this moment?

STUDENT ELLIS: Uh... I don't know... It could be any... That is, I'm not quite...

TUTOR SMITH: Ms Ellis, did you read the case we talked about yesterday?

STUDENT ELLIS: Yes! I read it – twice in fact. It involved the interpretation of Section 14(b) of the Race Relations Act.

TUTOR SMITH: If you've read it, *as you claim*, why are you unable answer the simplest question?

STUDENT ELLIS: (bursts into tears)

> University Law Departments have been described as a place for the accumulation of learning: First-year students bring some in; third-year students take none away. Hence, it accumulates.

The other practical problem with the Socratic method is that tutors who are either lazy or uninterested in teaching use it to kill time and avoid having to prepare a lecture:

TUTOR RYAN: Mr Lane, what did you think of the cases on this week's reading list?

STUDENT LANE: They were fine, I guess. Are you thinking of any one in particular?

TUTOR RYAN: Pick any one you want and tell us whether you agreed or disagreed with it?

STUDENT LANE: Well, I remember one that I thought made sense.

TUTOR RYAN: Good. Now, let's see… Ms Henson, do you agree or disagree with the case Mr Lane is referring to?

STUDENT HENSON: I'm not sure which one he's referring to.

TUTOR RYAN: Mr Lane, please explain the case to which you're referring, to Ms Henson.

This sort of thing is a far cry from the system that produced Plato. If Socrates were alive today, he'd be turning over in his grave.

Note: just because a tutor calls out your name doesn't mean you have to answer. If he doesn't know you personally (and he probably won't), just keep quiet and pretend you're not there – the 'foxhole' technique. The only problem is that students who do know you may give the game away by looking in your direction. If this happens, turn and stare intently at the person sitting beside you.

Law Students and Law Tutors

As a law student you will have to learn to deal with two sets of people: other students and tutors. The former have to be dealt with because they're physically ubiquitous – in the classroom, at the campus cafeteria, on that obscure library sofa where you were hoping to take a nap. The latter have to be dealt with because they're *psychologically* omnipresent, hovering about like superegos that speak in Latin.

Other Students

Although your fellow students will come in all sizes, colours, pedigrees and genders, they will fall into a few easily identifiable categories:

The Mainstreamer

Most of your classmates will have come straight from school to university and will be planning to go straight from university to law school. Some will have chosen their career out of driving ambition. Others will have been forced into it by their parents. Most will have done it because they couldn't think of anything else to do.

If male, the Mainstreamer's dress is conventional, his hair is short, his politics moderate to conservative and his personal habits unremarkable. If female, her dress is conventional, her politics mildly feminist and her willingness to have sex dependent on whether the relationship is 'meaningful'.

By and large, you will be able to understand and enjoy these people. The chances are that you are one of them.

The Keenie

Keenies are the most conspicuous as well as the most objectionable feature of university law departments. They have their hands in the air throughout lectures, manually pleading for an opportunity to discuss arcane points of law which they have discovered in *unrequired* reading. At the end of each class, they will bolt from their seats (invariably front and centre) to the podium, where they will collar the lecturer and further attempt to display their mastery of the obscure.

The psychology of the Keenie is pitiable. Deeply anxious and insecure, she degrades herself regularly by brown-nosing authority figures – not just lecturers and tutors, but law librarians, security guards and check-out crones in the campus cafeteria. The important fact to remember is that the Keenie's embarrassing behaviour reflects her internal problems, *not* the realities of passing a law degree. The Keenie is no more likely to get a 2:1 than you are.

You cannot always ignore the Keenie. Her excesses force their way into your life. But you should resist the temptation to solder a steel muzzle to her face.

Lecturers know how to deal with Keenies because every yearly intake has them. Keenies are as old as the law itself.

The Reformer

A number of your classmates will be 'mature' students who have taken up law out of pure economic necessity. Often they'll already have experience in social work, counselling, local government or some other field not renowned for its wealth-creating potential. They've switched to law because they think it will allow them to promote social reform *and* afford more than one Pot Noodle a day.

The Reformer has a hint of pathos about her, because she sees all too clearly that what would have been the next generation of philosophers, historians and scientists is being transmogrified into an army of litigators, corporate proofreaders and tax gurus. Don't feel too sorry for the Reformer, however. She may be disillusioned and subversive, but she represents strong competition.

LAW SCHOOL BINGO

This pastime is one of the most entertaining aspects of obtaining a law degree, and for this extremely limited purpose, the more Keenies you have in your lecture hall, the better. Before the lecture, someone distributes cards with the names of the most obnoxious Keenies laid out in a grid, like numbers on a Bingo card. Each card is slightly different. As given Keenies put their arms in the air to ask questions and are called upon by the lecturer, you cross their names off your card. The first person to cross out all the names on his card shouts 'Bingo!' and has won.

A word to the wise: if you should ever notice that yours is the waving hand whose recognition by the lecturer triggers a shout of 'Bingo!' consider whether your classroom conduct would benefit from a touch of restraint.

The Techie

The primary distinguishing feature of the Techie is that he did A levels in physics, chemistry or some other 'hard' science. You can recognise him by his bottle-bottom glasses and his ability to wear a brown, zipped cardigan and grey Hush Puppies without a trace of embarrassment.

The Techie used to hang round his university campus technology centre on Saturday nights to meet women. He did this every Saturday for three years, even though he never met any.

Law Tutors

Law tutors are a proudly idiosyncratic lot. Being as weird as you want is a major perk of academia, and some law professors wouldn't look out of place in the Addams Family. Nevertheless, like their students, law tutors fall into identifiable categories.

The Recognised Authority

Most law departments have at least one tutor recognised as a national or international authority on his subject – 'So-and-so on Company Law', 'That Other One on Evidence', 'Old whatsisname on Brain Death'. (The main difference between 'brain' death and ordinary death, by the way, is that with the latter you're not guaranteed a job with London Underground.)

There is only a chance correlation, if any, between status as a Recognised Authority and teaching ability. The Recognised Authority didn't attain that status by devoting lots of time to teaching. His lectures consist of 'Cases I advised on' and 'Lords of Appeal I call by their first names'.

Some Recognised Authorities with expertise in tax and other commercial areas maintain lucrative consulting contracts with big City firms in the 'one-day-per-week' to which their teaching contracts traditionally purport to restrict such activities.

Recognised authorities in less commercial areas such as civil procedure manage to convert their expertise into hard cash by publishing £50 casebooks that their classes are required to buy.

The Fuzzhead

Fuzzhead law tutors specialise in areas of breath-taking obscurity. They know absolutely everything there is to know about Road Traffic Law in Norman England, the Eritrean Law of Burial, Cremation and Exhumation or some other area no one else wants to touch (of which there are plenty).

The Fuzzhead may be brilliant, but the same escapist impulses that got him into his area of expertise render him unable to relate to other warm-blooded bipeds. He is a consistently miserable teacher, particularly when required to teach mainstream courses such as Contracts or Evidence. He should be avoided unless he has known propensities to mark generously – or unless you are of the Fuzzhead ilk yourself.

The Old Curmudgeon

The Old Curmudgeon is a classic feature of university law departments. Sometimes a former Recognised Authority grown irascible in his twilight years, he is dogmatic, demanding, impatient, crotchety and surly – on a good day.

The Old Curmudgeon conducts his classes like a regimental sergeant-major: you *will* attend all of his classes; you *will* be in your seat when he arrives; you *will* be prepared to discuss any case on the reading list.

The only way to deal with the Old Curmudgeon is gutless capitulation. If he accuses you of inadequate preparation, apologise for your craven stupidity. If he charges you with genetic idiocy, lament your forebears' reprehensible tradition of inbreeding.

Take comfort in the knowledge that the humiliation you risk by entering his class every day is no greater than that risked by your classmates. Take additional comfort in the knowledge that the Old Curmudgeon may not last another term.

The Young Star

Law departments are forever in search of the Young Star, someone short on years but long on the right credentials. Early publication of a highly acclaimed treatise, noted for its 'fresh outlook' and 'novel insights', is a sure sign of Young Star status. The fact that her proposals for reform have about as much chance of getting off the ground as an RAF Nimrod aircraft is immaterial.

The Young Star is a colourful figure on the law school campus, with her radical attitude, trendy clothes and preference for mixing with her students rather than the Common Room. Make the most of her refreshing outlook in a singularly dowdy branch of the teaching profession.

The Deadwood

Every law department has a few tenured members who don't do anything. In this respect they resemble big City firms. Deadwoods don't write articles, don't serve on law reform committees, don't do any private consulting and apparently don't prepare their lectures. No one is sure what they do with their time.

Rumour has it that some of them have very nice gardens.

The Entertainer

Many university law lecturers pride themselves on constituting the primary competition for Ricky Gervais. They like to think they can inject humour into even the most impenetrable legal subjects. The fact that they have all the wit and sophistication of Les Dennis on a bad day need not concern you. Watching someone failing to be funny is tremendously satisfying.

The problem with the Entertainer is not so much that he wastes time, though many do, but that students are lulled by his levity into thinking he'll be a generous marker, only to get their socks blown off in Finals. Enjoy the Entertainer, but don't slack up in his class any more than in your others. Keep your eye firmly on the ball for his Finals paper.

The Graduate Law Diploma (GDL) in a Nutshell

It's a regrettable fact that if you want to jump aboard the legal gravy train you've got to be standing on Platform 1 when it leaves town. Platform 2:1 will sometimes get you aboard. But the train from Platform 2:2 is the Oblivion Express heading non-stop to Nowheresville.

Another regrettable fact is that law exams, unlike many social science subjects, can't be tackled by writing pages and pages of what linguists and lexicographers often refer to as 'crap'. Bluffing your way through just isn't a realistic option. Most students realise this pretty quickly (some as many as three weeks before Finals) and hit the books like demons. They spend their every waking hour trying to ingest, in readily up-chuckable form, everything there is to know about certain 'core' subjects.*

---

* Many students ingest these materials at the same time they're ingesting their breakfast. Bear in mind that dried Bran Flakes, marmalade and toast crumbs on your textbooks substantially reduce their re-sale value.

Students also study a variety of non-core subjects – such as rapidly developing areas like Human Rights, Privacy or Environmental Law, increasingly marginal areas like Canon Law, or just plain non-existent areas, like International Law. But the core subjects are what your law degree is all about and, what's more, they're all a practising lawyer needs to know. The following sections set out all the key concepts and buzzwords of these subjects in clearer form than you'll ever get them in class.

Contracts

A passing familiarity with the law of contracts is all you need to hold yourself out as a 'commercial lawyer'. Leases, loan agreements, trusts, and lots of other documents with highfalutin' names are really just contracts. This should be borne in mind if another lawyer presents you with some document and you have no idea what it is. If it requires signing, and it isn't either a will or something that has to be filed in court, you can call it a contract without fear of being laughed at.

Offer and Acceptance
The entire law of contracts can be summed up in two words: *offer* and *acceptance*.

An offer is just what it sounds like: 'Hey, big guy, fifty quid for some action?'

So is an acceptance: 'Sure. But I want the cash up front.'

Whether a contract has been formed depends on whether

there has been a 'meeting of minds'. The acceptance must match the offer:

> JEREMY: Type up my thesis and I'll take you out to lunch.
> SARAH: No chance, pizza-face.

In that case, there was no meeting of minds. Sarah's reply did not match Jeremy's offer. No contract was formed.

Both offers and acceptances can be conditional:

> HENRY: I'd love to take you to the Coldplay concert – provided you get rid of that boil on your neck.
> ANGELA: Fair enough. I'll come with you, unless someone else – anyone else, really – asks me out – or in. Anywhere at all, really.

Consideration

Complicating the law of contracts is the concept of 'consideration'. The law won't enforce just any old promise. Consider this one: *'The next time I see you I'm going to give you a knuckle sandwich.'* The law will only enforce promises given in exchange for some return promise or equivalent sacrifice. The return promise or sacrifice is the *consideration* that makes the contract enforceable.

No one understands this concept. Why they call it *consideration*, when it has nothing to do with being nice to someone, is one of the law's well-shrouded mysteries.

Nevertheless, at least nominal consideration always has to be there. According to tradition, the delivery of a mere peppercorn is sufficient consideration for a contract to transfer the whole of the East End of London, complete with a 'Build your own Olympic Village' kit. (As a practical matter, of course, no one in their right mind would blow a whole peppercorn that way.)

That's why even multi-billion-pound contracts often start out with this bizarre recital: 'For £1 and other valuable *consideration*, we the undersigned hereby agree...'

At the close of the deal one of the lawyers may actually present the other side with a £1 coin (promptly recording it and billing it to his client with interest).

Breach

What if a client of yours breaches a contract? What if *you* breach a contract? Should you be embarrassed about it? Should your parents insist that you go through with it?

Not necessarily. In some instances the law *wants* you to breach your contract.

Suppose you've agreed to build a house for someone on a piece of land that turns out to have an interesting geological quirk: about 18 inches below the surface it harbours, well, a harbour, a body of water about the size of, say, the Irish Sea. Nobody knows why. All the geologists can say is that its surface is softer than the market for Japanese nuclear engineers. They say that if it retains any more water, it might be getting ready to have quintuplets. Do you have to proceed with the construction of the house, however futile it may be? No. The law doesn't see any point in you getting your feet wet, upsetting yourself, and taking it out on the dog just because of some silly old contract.

All the law requires is that you give the other party enough money to 'make him whole'. In deciding what would 'make him whole' a court would take into account such factors as the cost of building elsewhere, whether either party knew about the water under the land before signing, and perhaps the general unsavouriness of the parties involved.

Unenforceable Contracts

The law won't enforce certain categories of contracts, regardless of the presence of consideration, the absence of breach, or anything else.

One example is a contract which is deemed 'contrary to public policy'. Shylock's pound of flesh bargain would not nowadays be enforced south of the border (some Scottish courts remain very strict), and most courts would not require the loser of a bet on the Five Nations Cup to streak naked three times round Twickenham with a pound of sausages on his head.

The same is true of contracts made 'under duress'. A court would not require you to perform a contract that you accepted after Tony Soprano made you an offer you couldn't refuse. Of course, few such contracts actually make it to court. And if they do, there's no predicting how a judge will rule after receiving an offer to go swimming in Staines Reservoir in concrete Speedos.

A final category of contracts unlikely to be enforced involves contracts deemed 'unconscionable'. Occasionally a judge decides that a given contract is *so* unfair, so grossly one-sided, that there's no way he's going to enforce it. The theory seems to be that no sane and sober person would sign such a contract, and the stronger party must somehow have duped the weaker.

A classic example is the case of the old couple who bought a used Morris Marina (remember that beauty?) from a car dealer in Lewisham. The sale contract carried a disclaimer – in print so small it could only be read with the help of an electron microscope – saying that neither the dealer nor the manufacturer could be held liable for any injuries resulting from defects in the car.

When the steering wheel came off in the wife's hands as she was travelling along the A40 three days later, she ignored the disclaimer and sued.

Despite the disclaimer, the court ruled in her favour, saying the contract was unconscionable. It said that the average consumer has too little bargaining power in relation to big car companies, and the public interest in preventing bodily harm outweighs the presumption that a contract's terms should be enforced.

Liberals hailed the judge's decision in that case as a victory for natural justice. Conservatives denounced the judge as just one more do-gooder venting his sexual frustrations on the productive elements of society. The liberals were right; the contract wasn't made between two rational, free-acting parties. No one in his right mind would buy a Morris Marina from a used-car dealer in Lewisham.

The preceding case doesn't mean that you should get rid of all those unconscionable, illegible disclaimers in your Standard Terms of Contract. They serve an important 'dust-in-the-eyes' function, blinding the other party as to her actual rights. Also, they add incrementally to the length of the contract, thus adding incrementally to your client's mistaken but very valuable impression that you're doing a valuable job.

So go ahead and include a paragraph saying the purchaser acknowledges having inspected the power-steering system, even though she barely has the know-how to count the tyres. Add a provision to the effect that she personally supervised the assembly of the car stereo, even though it was made in China. For good measure, throw in a clause that prohibits her from rolling the windows up and down more than ten times a year.

The poor dodo won't be able to *find* these clauses, much less know they're legally meaningless. When she comes back to complain that the car has all the manoeuvrability of an oil supertanker (and worse mileage per gallon), that the radio only gets one channel (Radio Bogota), and that she tends to break a pretty hard sweat when she has to keep the car windows up even when it's 30°C outside, you can show her these clauses, and she'll go away.

Then all you'll have to worry about is whether you're going to burn in hell for your sins.

PALIMONY – A TRAP FOR THE UN-WEARY

Except in a few special situations, contracts need not be in writing to be enforceable. Oral agreements will do. In some instances, contracts need not even be spoken to be enforceable: a court may find an 'implied' contract based on the conduct of the parties.

The most common implied contract relates to co-habitees who split up – and the situation in which one of them sues the other claiming breach of an implied contract of ongoing support. This remains an uncertain area of law. It's basically a social question, one that turns on the mores of the day. What *are* the legitimate expectations of a woman who accepts an invitation to move in with a man for a couple of years? Is there necessarily a promise of support for life? What if he invites her over for just one evening – has he at least promised to buy her lunch next day?

And what if the tables are turned – she's a rich advertising executive and he's a starving artist who moves into *her* home? Does the whole thing depend on whether they had sexual relations? Should the result be different if he's impotent?

Advising clients in this area is very difficult, partly because the law is unsettled, but mainly because no one wants to take their lawyer along on a date.

For the time being, the best way to ensure safe sex is to supply your lecherous clients of all genders with blank waiver forms (see sample opposite) which they should have their prospective lovers execute at the first sign of lust – ideally before the first cocktail, and in any event before the Big Bang (a concept that persists in debauchery just as in astronomy.)

PALIMONY WAIVER
Between
The Stud [Insert Client's Name]
and
The Undersigned Prospective Lover
Period of Relationship covered by this Waiver: ....
(should not be less than 3 minutes)

The Lover, being of sound mind, nubile body, and substantial libidinous urges, hereby acknowledges the mutual nature of all pleasures and gratifications arising from any carnal relations, consummated or otherwise, between the Lover and the Stud, (said carnal relations hereinafter referred to as 'The Lust'), and hereby waives and disclaims any right(s) or entitlement(s) owing in connection with or arising from the Lust, whether such right(s) or entitlement(s) are of a physical, mental, financial, emotional, spiritual, existential, philosophical, subliminal, out-of-body, televised, or other nature.

Signed: .... (The Lover)

(In the Scottish Borders and parts of Cornwall, it is legally sufficient to place the Lover's hoof or paw print on the reverse of this form.)

Civil Procedure

'This above all: (a) To thine own self be true, and (b) never get to the merits of the case.' – Polonius, *Hamlet*

If you want to be a litigator, you need to know about 'civil procedure', which means the rules of court you have to follow when bringing or defending an action. The word 'civil' has nothing to do with politeness or using the proper fork. It differentiates the rules that apply to a 'civil' action from those that apply to a 'criminal' action. The latter are what you'll come up against if you stab someone, or hack into some celebrity's phone calls (unless you work for News International).

Civil procedure is easy. You just read the rules for whatever court you happen to be in, and follow them like recipes in a cook book: to start an action, you do A; to defend an action, you do B; if the other side lies, you do X; if your side lies, you do Y. In fact, there are only four concepts tricky enough to merit special attention:

Standing

'Standing' denotes a concrete personal interest in a legal action. It's something you've got to have in order to be heard in court.

Such an interest is easy to prove when you've been run over by an articulated lorry. Your broken legs give you standing. But what if you want to sue Parliament for passing a law that restricts fat people from hogging two-thirds of the sidewalk during lunch hour? If you're a willowy eight-stoner, you don't have standing because the law in question doesn't affect you personally. Even going out with a fat person isn't enough. This explains why you get six-year-old children as claimants in cases about, for instance, the adequacy of education services provided by a local authority. They haven't a clue what those people in suits are fighting about, but they've got to be the parties to the action, because they're the ones with standing.

Jurisdiction

The concept of jurisdiction determines which courts can hear which cases. To understand this, recall how things worked when you were a kid: 'Cases' about who should weed the garden probably fell within Dad's 'jurisdiction'; those involving whose turn it was to do the dishes probably fell within Mum's. If it wasn't clear who had jurisdiction, you engaged in 'forum-shopping' – you went to the one most likely to give you the answer you wanted. It's the same in law.

The basic jurisdictional rule is that small matters are heard in the County Court or Magistrate's Court, and more serious cases are heard in the High Court or the Crown Court. (Very small civil claims, i.e. those below £5,000, are heard in the Small Claims Court, in which no legal fees are recoverable.) There is an element of choice, however, and lawyers use it when possible. Lawyers would generally rather have their cases heard in the High Court or the Crown Court, partly because the judges are better, but mainly because of location and prestige. A lawyer who says he's going to the Old Bailey for a two-week trial is telling you he's a big shot. A lawyer who says he's going to Uxbridge Magistrates Court for the day is telling you where he's going.

Serving a Claim Form

Long before you can begin to explain to a court how you were sexually harassed by your lecherous boss, you have to give your boss notice of the action. She's entitled to defend herself.

You give her notice by delivering to her, or 'serving' on her, a copy of the Claim Form (formerly known as a 'writ'). Service of a Claim Form raises many practical questions. If you go to your boss's house and she won't open the door, how do you effect service? By placing it on her doorstep? Throwing it through her window? Beating her dog with it until she can't stand the pitiful howling and opens the door?

One option is to hire an independent agent. A private process server, usually a former bouncer or wrestler, will lurk in the shadows of her home until he catches her, invariably scaring her into a heart attack (see Torts, opposite).

The problem with private process servers is that they are not known for their reliability. The job doesn't pay that well and not many people enjoy lurking in the shadows of strangers' homes. They are renowned for tossing Claim Forms into the nearest skip or over canal bridges. Then they report back for payment. And because private process servers outweigh you by four stone, you pay up.

Class Actions

Contrary to what you might think, a class action isn't a dispute between people who wear Charles Tyrwhitt shirts, holiday in Mustique and adorn their living rooms with racing trophies. It is, put simply, a lawsuit with lots of people on one side or the other.

Class actions are increasingly common in this country now that the old rules against contingency fees have been swept away. Lawyers are now free to pursue their God-given right to go 'claimant-hunting' – which doesn't mean stalking a claimant, shooting him and mounting his body over your fireplace. For one thing, you'd never want more than the head. No, to go 'claimant-hunting' means to seek out a potential claimant and 'recruit' him to serve as your tool for siphoning funds out of the defendant's coffers.

In the United States, lawyers have this process down to an art form: wealthy corporate defendants (carefully selected on the basis of their tax returns, regulatory filings and sexually appealing CEOs) are delighted to settle before trial because they know juries will clobber them. (Juries love sticking it to executive big-wigs, for everything from corporate malfeasance to knowing what 'malfeasance' means.) And whenever a big class action settles, you can be sure that each side's lawyers go home with a new Rolls-Royce.

Now that UK law has caught up with the USA, a number of ripe, can't-miss class actions are just waiting to be litigated:

5 CLASS ACTIONS WAITING IN THE WINGS

1. An action against Simon Cowell on behalf of viewers of 'Britain's Got Talent' who now continually claim to be committed '250 per cent' to everything at every opportunity.

2. An action on behalf of all rail commuters who have tried a West Cornwall Pasty and ruined their clothes in a subsequent vomiting fit.

3. An action against Nabisco on behalf of all Shredded Wheat eaters who couldn't arm wrestle their grandmothers.

4. An action against Vivienne Westwood on behalf of all women who have bought one of her creations and realised that all they need is a squirting flower in their buttonhole to sign on with Zippo's Circus.

5. An action on behalf of all men who have bought *Lynx* and *still* not scored.

Torts

If you plan to hit the jackpot as a litigator, you need to master torts as well as civil procedure. Civil procedure tells you *how* to sue someone; torts tell you *what* to sue him *for*.

The first thing you need to understand in the area of torts is: what *is* a tort?

If someone stabs you, there are three ways he could get into trouble. First, the Crown Prosecution Service could prosecute him. Stabbing someone is a crime. It has been for years.

Second, if you and your assailant had previously exchanged promises not to stab each other, you could sue him for breach of contract. He *promised* not to do it.

Third, you could sue him for carving you up. You could demand payment for your medical bills, for your pain and suffering and for the cost of your prosthetic navel. But on what legal basis would you sue him? (You always need a legal basis.) He has committed a *tort* – in this case the tort of redesigning your anatomical landscape without your consent.

A tort is any misdeed you can sue someone for. Except breach of contract – that's called 'breach of contract'.

So if the *government* takes the case to court, it's a *crime*. If *you* take it to court, and there was no breach of contract, it's a *tort*.

Once you've got a handle on what a tort *is*, all you have to do to start an action is pick a tort – any tort. If you don't like the selection presently available, feel free to make up your own (explaining it to the judge as simply the next step in the law's manifest progression toward a more just and compassionate ordering of human relations).

The 'One-Bite' Rule

To get you going, consider a classic feature of tort law, the 'One-Bite' Rule. Normally a dog owner is allowed to let his dog run pretty freely about the place. This is considered unobjectionable because dogs are common domestic pets and usually don't bite people – unlike, say, a puffin, which must be securely leashed.

What if your adorable Great Dane, Chewy, tears a forty-stitch gash in your neighbour's right arm? Good old playful Chewy – *you* know he was just being affectionate. But your grumpy old neighbour (now called 'Lefty') doesn't see it that way. He's upset. Can Lefty sue you and win?

No. You were not *negligent*. You had no reason to think Chewy would bite anyone. You did not fail to act like that famous figure of tort law, the 'reasonable man'.

Lefty's gash is just his bad luck – like chewing gum on the bottom of your shoe, or being cornered by Nick Clegg at a party and being forced to listen to his plans for root-and-branch reform of the electoral voting system.

But what about Pit Bulls and Dobermans? They're known biters. In fact, they're considered so un-cuddly that they come under special statutory rules. And what about that German Shepherd that moved onto your street about the same time your cat disappeared? More important, what about Chewy, now that he has 'known vicious propensities'?

For dogs like Chewy, judges apply the 'One-Bite' Rule: after one bite, you're on notice that the dog is dangerous. If he bites again, you as owner can be held liable – and Chewy could face the ultimate sanction. (Actually, you've probably already done that to him. Now all we're talking about is putting him to death.)

The lesson for dog owners is clear. Don't squander that first bite on the postman. Make it count.

False Imprisonment

Another classic tort, a darling of law professors, is 'false imprisonment'. Contrary to what you might think, this doesn't refer to the situation in which baton-wielding riot police pounce on you, kettle you and your fellow demonstrators, throw you in the cells for a night, and charge you under the Public Order Act.

No, false imprisonment is what you sue young thugs for when they surround your car and won't let you out. False imprisonment could also be what Lefty sues you for when Chewy chases him up a tree and won't let him down until you call him in for a saucer of tea. The key is impairment of someone else's freedom of movement.

Law professors love to pose the following question: What if someone locks your door for several hours while you're asleep, so that you can't get out, but you don't *know* that you can't get out. Is that false imprisonment?

As an academic matter, who knows? Who cares? As a practical matter, if you have a client in this situation, go for it! Judges (famous for cat-napping) will identify with the sleeping party and be incensed at the thought of someone hanging around outside the door. They'll think 'What if I woke up and had to go to the lavatory?'

Habeus Corpus

Res Ipsa Loquitur

If you're going to get several new Bentleys because of someone's tort, you have to convince a judge that the tort actually happened. Usually you do this by eyewitness evidence: you get the old boy who was sleeping off six cans of Special Brew in a nearby alley to swear blind that the double-decker bus went through a red light at 70 mph when it hit your client's Mini.

But what if there were no eyewitnesses? What if the Special Brew drinker is so far gone that he can't get the story straight? All is not lost – you resort to the doctrine of *res ipsa loquitur*. This is Latin for 'the thing *(res)* speaks *(loquitur)* for itself *(ipsa)*'.

Note that the words are out of order. No wonder Latin is a dead language.

The case that gave rise to this doctrine involved a man who was walking along one day, minding his own business, when out of the blue he was hit on the head by a barrel of flour. He didn't see it coming. He didn't know where it came from. He just woke up in hospital covered with flour and ready to be deep-fried.

He sued the owner of the nearby flour warehouse, insisting that even though no one had seen it happen the owner or one of his employees *must* have negligently let the barrel fall out of the window. How else could the accident have happened?

He won his case. The judge said that in some cases the negligence is so clear from the circumstances that proof isn't necessary. He said, 'The thing speaks for itself.'

The only question is, why did he say it in Latin?

Causation
A final subject you need to understand if you're going be a specialist in tort law is the concept of causation.

Every event has millions of causes. Supposing your son Freddy is injured when he falls off the new bicycle you gave him for Christmas. Who or what *caused* his injury?

Did the bicycle company cause it by making a defective bike? Did the Local Council cause it by failing to fill in all those potholes that were often surrounded by tourists who mistook it for the Grand Canyon? Did Chewy cause it by leaping at Freddy with that 'dinner time' look in his eyes?

In theory, causation could be traced all the way back to Jesus of Nazareth for 'causing' you to celebrate Christmas.

The law has come up with the concept of 'proximate' causation to solve this difficulty. According to this doctrine, the most *immediate* cause is the one to which liability is assigned. Like most theoretical solutions to practical problems, proximate causation doesn't really help at all. It just gives judges a convenient label to apply to whomever they want to stick with the cost of the accident. In this case, the judge would probably decide that the bicycle company was liable – after all, it's the one with the money. Or, put more accurately, the one with an insurance policy that will pay up. In the end, most of these claims wind up being defended by insurance companies.

Real Property

Every lawyer should try to get to grips with the law of 'real property'. It takes some effort because it's a jargon-filled area that requires fluency in Olde English. When other lawyers try to intimidate you with terms like 'easement', 'seisin' and 'fee tail', you need to be able to come right back at them with 'frankalmoign', 'burgage tenure' and 'ousterlemain'. They won't know whether these terms are real; they don't know whether *their* terms are real. And it doesn't even matter. The point is *intimidation*. You have to show them you're not coming into this fight unarmed. *You've got game.* Once you've demonstrated that, you can get around to business.

Apart from anything else, understanding real property law is the only way to make sure that when you buy that sweet little weekend cottage in Somerset, you don't have 300 ramblers trampling over your flowerbeds every Sunday afternoon.

Real property comprises two types of things: (1) Land, earth, soil, dirt – everything along these lines except what your potted plant is sitting in, and (2) 'Fixtures' i.e. buildings and other items so large, heavy or immobile as to be virtually part of the land. This latter category would include darts professionals and your last five blind dates.

You then have to apply the right labels to these two things: for example, if someone sells you a farmhouse with 10 acres of land, you don't just say it's your land; you say that you hold a *fee simple absolute in possession*.

And if you want to give a plot of that land to your brother's children (your own children bear an unsettling resemblance to your wife's personal trainer, the guy known around the gym as Alex the Wonder Horse), you don't just scribble your instructions on the back of an envelope. You've got to go through all the right procedures to convey a *fee tail interest in the land*.

There are scores of these kinds of labels. They don't make sense. They don't sound like anything you've ever heard of. You've just got to memorise them.

Squatter's Rights

A peculiar but important concept of real property is that you can acquire valid legal title to a piece of land simply by taking it and holding on to it for a long time. This method of acquiring title is known as 'adverse possession'.

It isn't quite as easy as it sounds. First you have to possess the land, and your possession of it must be 'actual'. If you decide you'd like three feet of your neighbour's garden to square off your croquet lawn, it's not enough to just *proclaim* that the three feet are yours. You have to put up your hoops and start playing.

Second, your use must be 'open' and 'hostile'. You can't just sneak onto the lawn at night, wearing dark clothes and a black balaclava, and have a friend snap a flash photo to prove you were there. And you can't trick your neighbour by telling him you're just borrowing the land for a while, like a cup of sugar. You have to be claiming it's *yours*. Guard dogs and razor wire would help satisfy this requirement.

Third, your use of the land has to be 'exclusive'. If other neighbours are trying to get in on the act by, say, growing tomatoes on the plot you're trying to claim, you lose. So do they, for the same reason, unless tomatoes are out of season.

Fourth, you have to use and be in possession of the land 'continuously'. If you want it that badly, and you're too cheap to pay for it, cancel your world cruise. Scratch your tour of duty with the Foreign Legion. Forget your hopes of presenting *Vacation, Vacation, Vacation*. You've got to *be* there.

Finally, you have to hold the land and satisfy all these other requirements for many, many years. This is the hard part. This is what keeps you from pitching your tent on your neighbour's lawn with the intention of fighting him off tooth and nail until title changes hands – this and the fact that if he calls the police, you'll spend the night in the clanger.

If you *could* fulfil all these requirements, your neighbour's lawn could be yours. You could leave him singing the adverse possession blues.

With the right tactics, and a bit of patience, you could take over the whole of South Kensington. How do you think the Grosvenors got Mayfair?

The Rule against Perpetuities

The most irritating feature of real property law is the Rule against Perpetuities. You know that fabulous farm in Devon where your father grew up? Or that super piece of undisturbed beachfront on the Isle of Wight where you've holidayed for years and that you intend to keep in the family forever? You can't do it. The Rule against Perpetuities won't let you.

First announced in 1681, the Rule provides that: '*A contingent future interest which, by any possibility, may not vest within twenty-one years after some life in being, is void in its inception.*'

The main point, according to modern theologians, is that no one should be able to control a piece of land forever. This means that even if you think St Paul's Cathedral ought to remain a national monument till the end of time, people in the year 2500 should be able to convert it into a raw sewage plant if they want to.

The Rule against Perpetuities has inspired endless pages of discussion – pages that would have been more usefully employed on perforated rolls in motorway service stations.

If you were studying the Rule in your degree course, this is the sort of question you might get:

The following provision appears in your father's will. Who gets the land, for how long, and can he raise pigs on it?

'*A makes a gift to B for the life of C, remainder to D's heirs, so long as D has heirs, but if C's first born should be ginger haired, then to E's heirs, so long as B's grandchildren may reside in Lincolnshire, then to such heirs of B as may survive the then living residents of Broadmoor – on Thursdays.*'

You would have two minutes to answer this question.

CHAPTER 4

SUMMER PLACEMENTS

Flattery and deception

Lots of law students spend part of their summer holidays on a placement – sometimes called a 'vac scheme' – with a law firm. Summer placements are not unlike teenage black-tie balls, where you dress like an adult, drink like an adult, and try to get your end away like an adult – only to realise later that it is about as close to real life as Eddie the Eagle was to an Olympic gold medal. Oh yes, summer placements *resemble* private practice, but there are significant differences of which you should be aware.

Socially, they can be pleasant indeed. Most firms, particularly the large ones, wine and dine their summer students like visiting dignitaries. In the good old days these extravaganzas were on a par with anything Caligula's party-planners ever served up (except the sex parts; law firm party planners have always been ahead of Caligula's on that front). In these difficult times, though, it's pretty much BYOC (bring your own concubine). Still, you'll be treated to some excellent food, and the whole thing is a gigantic freebie.

The ulterior purpose of this utterly misleading display of largesse is to stimulate a serious lust for lucre in the corruptible heart of the typical law student and to blind him to the rather grimmer reality of private practice.

As a PR routine it contains elements of both the comical and the fraudulent. It's comical because of the disparity between the students' actual contribution to the work of the firm and the attention accorded them; few summer students do enough useful work to actually pay their way, and *no* summer students command the actual respect of the partners.

It is fraudulent simply because it is unrealistic. The conviviality and the largesse is a seasonal phenomenon, lasting a few short weeks in the summer, but conspicuously absent the rest of the year. Ask yourself why that partner who strolls through the library says a cheerful hello to you but totally ignores the full-time associate on the next desk. Does the partner not remember the associate's name? Did he know his name when he was a summer student? Did something change when he signed on permanently?

Most law students save a few weeks at the end of the summer to travel or work on their tans. This is understandable but unfortunate, because that is when you could get your most realistic look at a firm. By then, the regulars are sick of playing host to presumptuous university undergraduates, and the facade of rah-rah enthusiasm collapses. The result is normality – grim, ugly normality. If possible, stick around a while longer – it'll be an eye-opener.

Professionally, as well as socially, summer placements depart from reality. Most firms engage in 'cream-skimming', i.e. reserving for summer students all the interesting projects around the office (a big firm may have two or three in a summer). This is why so many summer students are later surprised to find that being a trainee offers about as much dignity and satisfaction as sweeping Earls Court after the Horse of The Year Show.

Firms compound the fraud by ignoring mistakes by summer students that, if committed by a full-time associate, would mean the loss of her job or even her Dictaphone. This may sound like good news as far as the student is concerned, but in reality it's a mixed blessing:

Unless you make a serious hash of things – like misspelling a partner's name in a memo – all you'll be told is that your work was excellent, everyone liked you, and the firm wants you back. Then, at whichever firm you end up with, you'll naturally return to the patterns and practices that served you so well over the summer, only to discover – *after* the black marks are permanently engraved on your record – that those patterns and practices are about as acceptable as white socks and lizard skin brogues. But then it's too late. You're a dead man not walking. You couldn't be resurrected even if your name was Lazarus and your best friend walked on water.

CHAPTER 5

THE LEGAL PRACTICE
COURSE (LPC)

*Thousands of morons have
passed it. So can you!*

The first decision you confront after graduating with a law degree is whether or not to take up that place at law school you reserved seemingly aeons ago. A few slackers postpone the decision for a year on the grounds that if they don't get Thailand out of their system now, they never will. (Known phonetically as the 'Phu Ket! I'm going...' career move.)

Others indulge the hope of avoiding the Legal Practice Course (or LPC) altogether by going straight into teaching.

The wiser course is to bite the bullet and take the course, if for no other reason than to be able to tell your parents you're finally equipped to get a proper job.

It's not as if passing the LPC requires great intelligence. Even if you're so brain-dead that all you need for survival is direct sunlight and watering twice a week, you still have a good chance of passing. If you doubt this, stroll down to your nearest Magistrates Court and check out the first solicitor you meet.

Passing Finals *does* require one thing: a decent memory. There's a load of material to read – some casebooks come with wheels – and success in the exam has a lot to do with being able to regurgitate large amounts of material under pressure. In the end, quantity triumphs over quality.

The position is aggravated because most of the rules you learn are completely arbitrary. For example, either you know the order of distribution of a limited partnership's assets, or you don't. An ability to *think* is irrelevant. For something like that you've just got to sit down and memorise it.

Not that you need to memorise *every*thing. Your goal is to pass, not to get the highest grade ever given. 'MCE' should be your guide: Minimal Critical Effort. The ideal grade is the absolute lowest pass given to anyone in your year.

You will hear stories of people who spent all summer windsurfing in Cannes, glanced at the textbooks on the flight home, and then breezed through the exams. Such stories fall into the same category as the Monster Raving Loony Party manifesto: appealing but ultimately unrealistic. You have to give the LPC *something*.

What if you fail? Failing the LPC is not the end of the world. It will feel like that, however, because it will indeed be the end of *your* world, at least in every meaningful sense. Let's start with the little things. If you still have any money after the other things that happened to you immediately after you failed, you'll have to fork it over for the Round 2 retakes. And you'll be taking them in mid-Winter when there won't be a lot of skimpy summer clothes and nice tans to keep your morale up (as if you'll have any morale to keep up after a failure of this magnitude).

Don't worry about how to break the news to everybody. The whole world will already know. The national newspapers publish the names of everybody who has passed, and people (especially relatives) pore over the list the same way they pore over the fatalities from a major train crash, as interested in the names that *aren't* on it as in those that are. (The big difference between being in a major train crash and failing the

COPING WITH FEAR: CONTINUE TO WRITE

You don't have to be a naturally timid person to experience fear during LPC final exams. You can easily pick it up from someone else.

Fear is contagious. When the person next to you starts emitting regular and powerful rectal sobs, you may find your own stomach begins to churn. This is understandable, like the feeling you get when the pilot of your aeroplane emerges from the cockpit strapping on his parachute.

Suppress your feeling of panic. Continue to write. Whatever happens, continue to write. If your neighbour has a heart attack, continue to write. If you have a heart attack, try to tough it out until the invigilator calls an end to the exam. If you can't last that long, be sure to gasp loudly or wave your arms to catch the invigilator's attention because those around you with any sense will carry on writing.

You should also studiously ignore those other banes of the exam hall — the smirkers. These are the people who spend at least ten minutes of each hour trying to catch the eye of other candidates so that they can convey, by their expressions, what they think of the exam paper.

If they could tell you the answers it would be one thing, but they can't. All they can do is put the wind up you. Supposing you're happy with the way things are going and you receive a look that says: 'What did we do to deserve this?' You'll start to wonder what you've missed. Why are you finding it so easy, when brain box Carter has just told you he's struggling? Have you misread the instructions?

If, on the other hand, you've read every question on the paper three times and still can't find one you can write more than a paragraph on, and you receive a look that says 'what a gift!' it may activate latent psychopathic tendencies, which won't do your career any good at all.

LPC is that the train crash victims die quickly, and without personal humiliation – unlike people who fail these tests.)

So how can you avoid failing? Follow this one golden rule: don't panic! People seem to get unusually nervous about their LPC exam – not, of course, without good reasons: the physical environment is unfamiliar, the people around you are strangers, and you're too smart not to realise that failing here means failing everywhere, for the rest of your life, and soon you will have no work, no friends and no clothing, and you will starve to death on the street, cold, alone, hungry (even in death) and naked. And then dogs will urinate on you.

So relax.

If you think about it, there's no actual reason to panic. You've taken hundreds of exams before, passed all or most of them, or quite a few, and these are different only in length and the fact that failure could result in disgrace and painful death – and not only for you, but also for your children, and for the children *they* would have had if you hadn't failed and humiliated them beyond what anyone can bear.

So relax.

If you feel a wave of panic about to come over you, try to nip it in the bud. Slap yourself hard and remind yourself that you have never failed an exam in your life, not one as important as this one, anyway. The slap should also remind you of what happened when you got a little frisky with your roommate several years ago, and how embarrassing that was, and how failing this exam will be eighty-five times worse, so you'd better get yourself together and relax.

Now, if you *have* failed an exam in your life, remind yourself that no one has ever been jailed for failing the LPC. First offenders usually get a suspended sentence, because what's the point when you're going to die soon anyway?

At the end of the seventh day, when the final 'Put down your pens' has been called, you will feel giddy, like a marathon runner crossing the finishing line.* This is partly because of all the nervous energy you will have expended. You may also have forgotten to eat for several days. At this point you should do three things:

First, go home and get some sleep. Fatigue contributes to depression. When you wake up, you will have only the vaguest memories of the agony you have been through.

Actually, that's absurd. You'll re-live every second of it, over and over, for months, at times moaning, at other times shrieking, always with nausea, cramps and diarrhoea. But, if you're stupid enough to believe something like that, go ahead and tell it to yourself. No harm in it – if, again, you're stupid enough to believe it.

Second, resist talking about the exam. If you still need to be told this after all these years, you really are a loser. View this as one last chance to redeem yourself. (Besides, people will know how you did soon enough, and then your life could be on the downhill slide, so why subject yourself to more torture than you might very well experience in a month or two anyway?)

Third, take as long a holiday as you can possibly afford. Once you start work, you may not have a similar opportunity for decades. And since there's always a chance you *won't* start work, because you failed, why not take some time now to see parts of the world that you might never again have a chance to see, not because you won't have time – you'll have all the time in

---

* You may also smell a bit funny — the analogy with the marathon runner is again apt.

the world – or because you'll be penniless, although you might in fact be penniless, but because you might die.

You will not get your results for three or four months. The inherent horribleness of this delay will be exacerbated by rumours about lost exam papers, unprecedented failure rates, and cheating scandals that require everyone to take the exam again. Ignore these rumours. The same ones surface year after year – apparently by spontaneous generation (a view propagated by Creationists).

The important thing to remember is that you will eventually pass. If not the first time, the second. If not the second, the third. Actually, of course, it's entirely possible that you'll never pass it – *ever* – especially if you've already failed it twice, because it's well established that people who've failed it twice are numb nuts.

But suppose you pass it, the first time or, against all odds, the second: what you really need to worry about is what comes after that.

14 PRACTICAL SKILLS THEY OUGHT TO TEACH YOU IN LAW SCHOOL – *BUT DON'T*

1. Faking interest during interviews.
2. Not believing 90 per cent of what they tell you when you do a summer placement at a firm.
3. Masking your delight at the size of your first pay slip.

4. Masking your disappointment at the size of your twenty-fifth pay slip.

5. Dealing with sexual advances by senior lawyers.

6. Dealing with sexual advances by motorbike couriers.

7. Sucking up to secretaries and other support staff.

8. Pretending you don't think your clients are stupid.

9. Sleeping with your eyes open. (Hey, fish do it.)

10. Not worrying about the cost to your client.

11. Generating excuses for monumental errors.

12. Mediating between your brain's craving for coffee and your bowels' craving for peace.

13. Pretending you don't hate everyone at your firm.

14. Pretending you don't regret going into law.

CHAPTER 6

RECRUITING

*I spent £500 on a new suit
just to meet this creep?*

Time was when a law student could stroll into Slaughter & May on a Friday afternoon, say 'so, what can you lot do for me?' and, provided the stud in her nose wasn't too obvious, she'd be behind her desk on Monday morning. Career mistakes were that easy to make.

Those days are but a distant memory. Training contracts are now scarcer than a taxi-driver's thank you, with many qualifiers chasing each vacancy. And it's going to get worse before it gets better.

In such a competitive climate, success and failure depends as much on interpersonal skills as academic ability. And the crunch comes at interview time. You can't afford to breeze in and out of an interview any more, treating the first two or three tiddlers as warm-ups for the biggies at the end. You can't rely on your natural charm, wit and evident intelligence to pull you through when the questioning gets tough. Look at yourself in the mirror – you're wearing a tie, for God's sake. (Even if you're female.) What does this tell you? You're not in school anymore. An interview is a *test* – the sternest, most intensive test of all. So do your homework. And straighten up your room afterwards, the way your mother taught you.

Because let's face it: getting a job is what it's all about. Not many people go to law school because they can't think of anything else to do with their money.

Interviews have a lot in common with family weddings. Both involve forced smiles, frequent handshakes, questions no one cares about the answers to, and a radical departure from normal behaviour. Play along. This doesn't make you a hypocrite or a sell-out. It means you're baiting the hook to catch the fish. Go dig up some worms.

The way you present yourself to a City firm which specialises in advising major financial institutions and mega-rich private clients, is going to be very different from the way you present yourself to firms that specialise in criminal and personal injury work on behalf of legally aided clients. Lawyers in these two types of firms have gone into law for entirely different reasons: one to make money, the other to atone for strong feelings of guilt. (These feelings no doubt originated in something appalling, something that would have Dr Freud himself cringing in astonishment.) And, since recruiters invariably recruit in their own image, your strategy should be to mirror the attitudes and appetites of whomever you're talking to. (Unlike the forced smiles and frequent handshakes discussed above, *this* is hypocritical. But there's a way to deal with that: ignore it.)

If you don't know anything about the interviewer's firm – and there's really no excuse for this, unless you got lucky last night, which is recognised as a good excuse by every land-based mammal on the planet – take note of the location of its offices. That can tell you a lot, because firms tend to group around their client base: entertainment law firms usually plant their flags in the West End, technology firms prefer the M4 corridor, and white collar crime firms get as close as possible to the investment banks.

But whichever kind of firm you want to work for, there are common ground rules to observe if you want to get the job.

The main rule to bear in mind is that law firms, like lemmings, have no independent sense of judgement. They want you if they think their competitors want you. They're less interested in your credentials than in how their competitors view your credentials. Ergo your basic goal is to make them think that other leading firms have already made you an offer or are on the verge of doing so.

This doesn't mean you actually have to lie (although worrying about that after three years of law school is just plain weird). You can achieve the desired effect simply by dropping the names of other big firms into the conversation – what you think of Herbert Smith's training programme; how Mayer Brown's fancy new offices struck you; why you're not sure whether Linklaters is for you. If anyone asks if these firms have actually made you an offer, just say you 'don't feel at liberty to discuss that right now'. If that feels weird, you could say you haven't heard from them yet – which is surely true if you never even sent them a CV.

In order to get a job at a law firm, you'll probably have to survive two types of contact: the on-campus screening and the full-scale assault at the firm's offices. Each of these stages calls for different strategies and techniques.

The On-Campus Screening

Many of the big firms send delegations to give a presentation at what they regard as the acceptable universities: Oxford and Cambridge. Some of them make a self-conscious effort to broaden the intake by visiting Bristol, too. If you're at some third-rate former polytechnic, forget it. Don't even squander the cost of postage to mail them your CV.

Assuming you attend one of these presentations, what should your tactics be? Bear in mind that the room is likely to be full to the brim with other finalists equally desperate to make an impression – first-year students hoping for free booze, and a student band rehearsing the tunes they'll be playing on the London Underground when they can't land a job.

In such circumstances the conventional approach will not work. Thrusting your CV into a visiting partner's hand when he's already trying to balance a wilting paper plate of cocktail sausages, a glass of wine and half a buttered baguette, will only serve to irritate. Neither is this the occasion to dazzle him with stories of your academic triumphs.

What this is the occasion for is scoring big points on *personal style*, rather than any substantive qualities.

This means more than wearing matching shoes, doing your flies up and remembering the name of the firm in which you're supposedly eager to spend the rest of your professional career – important as those things are. (If you show up in leisurewear and a Bob Geldof haircut, you might as well make the most of the free food, because that's all you're ever going to get out of that firm.)

It means being distinctive, memorable. It means not boring the hell out of the visiting partner with weak questions that (a) you should already know the answers to ('How big is your firm?'), (b) the partner couldn't care less about ('Does the child-care voucher entitlement increase in line with inflation?'), and (c) show you're labouring under some terrible misapprehension ('Is it right that the top priority of Magic Circle law firms is corporate responsibility?').

It means asking questions not about the firm, but about the visiting partner personally ('Did you have any expectations when starting at the firm that weren't met?'), so he'll have an opening to talk about the subject that interests him most, i.e. himself. The applicant who does this is invariably remembered as 'a stimulating, thoughtful conversationalist'.

Do some homework on the firm in advance so that you can impress the partner with the incisiveness of your questions. All law firm websites now have lists of partners and their areas of practice.

If you know which partner is going to be visiting, try to find out a bit about him, and drop complimentary references to his university, his place of birth and the year he was born.

But be diplomatic with this 'informed' approach. The partner won't enjoy talking about the recent indictment of his senior partner on insider dealing charges, nor will he care to speculate on his son's chance of parole.

Finally, if you have any choice in the matter, try to attend a presentation early on in the recruitment season, when the visiting partners are still feeling fresh and not like they're going to throw up if they see one more eager beaver in a new suit who really has no idea what he's getting into.

The Formal Interview

The most important thing to remember about the formal interview is to go easy on the coffee and the tea. Quite apart from the fact that you may be too nervous to hold the cup steadily, every firm will offer you some and you simply cannot win the battle of the bladder.

Otherwise your strategy should be pure *How to Win Friends and Influence People*: talk about whatever your interviewers find most interesting. For lawyers, this means talking about themselves.

It isn't hard to get them going. Ask them what kind of law they practise, how long they've been at it, what got them into it. Lawyers love contemplating their origins and destinies.

Towards the end of the interview, throw in a question or two about the firm and its excellent reputation, just to show you're

GROOMING YOURSELF FOR INTERVIEW

This is one of the trickier areas we'll get into, because there's a limit to what you can do if, say, your face doesn't fit. We're using 'fit' broadly here; it may be that what your face doesn't fit is the interviewer's expectations. Alternatively, maybe it doesn't fit the rest of your body. A third possibility is that your face doesn't fit within the limits of human tolerance for the decaying and hideous. In any event, you might have the best legal brain of your year, but if something in your appearance gives the impression you're about to offer your interviewer £2,000 worth of the leading export commodity of Bogota, he'll get nervous.

Nevertheless, there are various elements of appearance and posture that you should be aiming for. With work and a bit of practice, you can get surprisingly good results from even the most unpromising physical material.

Eyes

Must be purposeful and thoughtful, with just the right number of blinks per minute. If you blink too often, you'll come over as a bit of an oddball and be deemed unpresentable to the firm's clients; if too seldom, you'll remind them of Hannibal Lecter – an even less acceptable proposition. Eye colour is less important, as most people don't notice anyway; blue-grey is probably the ideal, but anything other than cockerel-orange will do.

Mouth

Short of dribbling onto your tie or leering like Russell Brand, you should be alright with whatever kisser God gave you. If you plan to be a litigator, however, add a hint of ruthlessness to your appearance by occasionally pursing your lips in a rather cruel thin smile. Remember the 'rather', and choose your moment carefully: if you do it just after the interviewer has commented '*Sussex University, huh — you must have been there when they had that serial rapist prowling around campus*', you may end up getting early experience of the Police and Criminal Evidence Act.

Complexion

If you've picked up a tan in the course of your summer revision, powder your skin before going in for your interview. Law firms have a strong aversion to tans, which they've heard are acquired by doing unnatural things, such as going outside. Remember: in the law, photosynthesis is for plants, not fee-earners.

If on the morning of your interview you're looking just too damn drop-dead hunky, take immediate action. Try shaving with a bread knife, or chew some cordite in the train. It will instantly render your skin an off-putting, lawyerly grey.

Expression

Decisive, authoritative, cynical, manipulative, calculating — these are some of the characterisations you should aspire to. A tall order for one face, granted, especially while tackling Eyes and Mouth at the same time, so take it slowly. Start with a couple at a time, and work your way up.

a serious player. You'll strike a particularly responsive chord if you inject references to 'billings' or 'profits' – anything related to money.

If you find yourself short of conversation, personalise the discussion a bit. He may have a framed picture of himself and some celebrity client on the wall. Ask him how he got to know Jamie or Cheryl or Kerry. He won't be irritated by your impudence. Why do you think the pictures are on the wall in the first place?

On the other hand, you're probably better off *not* complimenting the old geezer on the lovely picture of his granddaughter sitting on his desk – it could turn out to be his fourth wife.

If you're being interviewed by an associate rather than a partner (it's amazing how seldom partners participate in the recruiting process), the rules are rather different. Don't bother asking about the firm at all. He has probably just put down an armful of legal documents with pages numbering in three figures. The last thing he wants to talk about is more law.

Most interviews tend to take place in meeting rooms, but in case you're invited into the inner sanctum of the associate's office, take note of its trappings. The things he has on display are things he likes to talk about, things he's proud of. If he has an oar hanging on the wall, ask him if by chance he ever crewed an eight at university. (Be sure to say 'crewed an eight' rather than 'rowed a boat'. Rowers are a quaint breed and very particular about their terminology.)

If, on the other hand, he's a dead ringer for Mr Puniverse, steer the conversation towards 'safe' subjects like bidding conventions in contract bridge, or your long-held ambition to holiday with the Navajo Indians. Chances are he'll have similar interests.

At some point in the interview, express curiosity as to whether the partnership recognises the talents of its star associates (including, by clear implication, the one you're talking to). Every associate feels underappreciated, and this comment will render you instantly likeable in his eyes.

The Recruiting Lunch

Sometimes the recruiting ritual includes being taken out to an expensive lunch. When you're an indigent student, this can be a major occasion – your first square meal in weeks, as well as your first taste of legal largesse.

If you're in the right frame of mind, a recruiting lunch can be a lot of fun. Your escorts will usually be associates rather than partners, and they will generally strive to take full advantage of the outing to enjoy themselves and run up a hefty bill at the partners' expense. Don't be so churlish as to decline their offers of lightly chilled Chablis and the largesse of the firm's partners.

One reason you should encourage them to drink heavily is that a recruiting lunch can be an opportunity to get the truth about a firm, depending on how many drinks the associates have had and whether they're the sort who feed on one another's gripes: 'You think *you* got shafted by that partner, listen to what the bastard did to *me* last week…' Encourage them to continue in this vein, it'll be a revelation.

If they offer you a drink, do you accept? Of course you do – *you* don't have to go back to work. This is especially true if your hosts are already behaving like Sharon Osbourne on the *X Factor*. You don't want to appear a stick-in-the-mud.

What should you order? This is not the time to play 'Stump the Barman'. Order wine – it's posher than alcopops. And don't look surprised when the waiter asks if you want red or white. Wine always comes in colours – but not beige, cream or duck egg blue.

Don't feel guilty about the cost of the meal, and for God's sake don't try to minimise the bill by under-ordering. It's not *your* fault they're trying to impress you, and you can bet they won't thank you for lowering the ante by ordering the cheapest pasta dish on the menu. Just view it as part of your reward for accumulating a good record. Besides, whatever firm you end up with will extract recompense soon enough.

RECRUITING LUNCH DISASTERS

No matter how relaxed a recruiting lunch may seem, remember that you are constantly on trial. Don't try to be funny, by for example unscrewing the top of the salt cellar and offering it to your host, no matter how many rounds of applause that particular stunt won you in your campus refectory. And beware these common mistakes:

- At a Chinese restaurant, don't blow your nose on the pancakes that come with the Peking duck.

- At an Italian restaurant, don't order spaghetti Bolognese or any other dish likely to get friendly with the front of your shirt.

- At *any* restaurant, avoid exotic dishes like cat or raw boa-constrictor. Only seriously deranged litigators at Herbert Smith are expected to enjoy this — and then only on the eve of a major court case.

- Resist the temptation to pop one of those round yellow tasty-looking things into your mouth, because it is probably a rolled-up butterball. If you do make this mistake, do not attempt to rescue the situation by declaring, 'Now *that's* what I call a good butterball.'

> • If the bill passes within your visual range, do not let out a long low whistle and exclaim, 'Hey, I didn't know we broke a window!'

Your Curriculum Vitae

Don't waste your time producing a flashy CV. Lawyers are not aesthetic enough to appreciate good packaging and they view a really slick-looking CV with scepticism, even scorn. They just aren't into glitz; they're into drab – which they think allows them to be people of substance rather than mere form.

What they're really interested in are your exam results. Occasionally they might consider other achievements, especially those showing an unusual ability to stomach huge piles of grunt work. Being a proofreader at the Sanskrit Publishing Centre would qualify, as would spending your summer holidays shovelling stable strudel at your local riding school. These kinds of activities say something about your suitability for private practice.

So, if your exam results are good, put them front and centre. That's obvious. The more difficult problem is what to do with them if they're awful? What if the only A-grade you got was in one of those touchy-feely social science subjects where *everybody* got an A, because the bearded tree-hugger who taught it didn't like passing negative value judgements?

That's a tricky one. Your interviewer isn't just passing the time when he asks about your exam results. If yours are dreadful, you have two options: the first is to look him in the eye and assert with cool confidence, 'These marks don't reflect what I can do' – and hope they fall for it. (Be sure to say '*these* marks' rather than '*my* marks' – the goal is to disassociate yourself from them, as if they were somebody else's.)

The other option is to look him in the eye and assert with cool confidence, 'My father is a rich and powerful man. He'd be very pleased – indeed, eager to repay your generosity – if you took me on'.

History suggests that the second is the more effective ploy.

Note two items that should not be included in your CV. First, in describing a previous summer placement (if you've done one, and maybe even if you haven't), don't bother saying 'Researched and drafted memoranda and performed other litigation tasks'. Lawyers know what summer students do – and it's not impressive enough to warrant elaboration.

Second, don't clog up the personal section of your CV with things like 'Health: Excellent'. Law firms don't care about your health. Take a look at the people interviewing you, with their paunches, skinny arms and pasty complexions. Is *their* health excellent?

The Covering Letter

All a covering letter needs to say is 'Here's my CV. Got a job?' You can dress it up a little with the more formal 'Enclosed is my CV…' language, but forget the stuff about how you're applying to the firm 'because it has a varied, high-profile practice that you believe would offer a stimulating and challenging introduction to a career in the law'.

Cut to the chase. You don't have to sell them on their own firm.

If you have something to say, say it in your CV rather than in the covering letter – with a few rare exceptions, such as that your mother speaks well of their firm, and she should know because she's their biggest client.

Photos

Sometimes firms ask you to attach a passport-sized photo to

your CV. This is so they can identify you at reception, and it has nothing to do – do you hear me? *Nothing to do* – with wanting to check your race, sex or class before inviting you in for interview.

Sure.

Do what they say, anyway. Spend an afternoon and fifty quid or so in a Photo-Me booth trying to get something vaguely acceptable. In that first elimination stage, where one hundred CVs make it straight into the 'No' letter tray, and ten go through to the next round, a lot will depend on whether you look the part.

Don't go over the top by, for instance, getting a professional to take a posy shot of you reading War and Peace in your gazebo, galloping on your pet camel over the South Downs ('That was taken during my Lawrence of Arabia period'), or staring wistfully into the sunset. Not unless you want to become the recruiting office pin-up. Firms aren't looking for 'mood'. They're looking for something forensic, something that will allow them to tell how much alcohol you're likely to have in your bloodstream on a Monday morning, and whether you'll flip when told to cancel your honeymoon to help do the final proofreading on a big flotation.

Recruiting Misrepresentations

Law firms, like second-hand car dealers, are known for their willingness to misrepresent reality. Their recruitment brochures often deviate so far from the truth as to constitute what most people would call 'lies'.

Lies told by law firms and car dealers are not punishable under the law. They're known as 'mere puffs'. Examples of mere puffing by car salesmen would be 'There will always be a strong resale market for the Rover 200' and 'The Reliant Robin is well-known for its road-holding'. Below are some of the most common recruiting lies, each translated into what recruiters *would* say if they were burdened by a proclivity for the truth.

What Recruiters *Say*	What Recruiters *Mean*
Our associates work hard, but like it.	Our associates work hard.
You'll get an excellent training at this firm.	At the end of your training, no one will have better pagination skills.
We have one of the more diversified practices in the City.	We'll take any work that comes in the door.
We believe in lean staffing of cases.	We make each associate do the work of three.
We don't spend the entire day in the office.	We take a lot of work home.
Our lawyers maintain a variety of outside interests.	Three years ago we had an associate whose wife played the piano.
This firm likes to keep a low profile.	Nobody has ever heard of us.
We encourage pro bono work.	We tolerate pro bono work on weekends.
We believe in bringing trainees along one step at a time.	You'll be indexing court documents for months (and we define a 'month' as what you call a 'year').
We have a policy of carefully controlled growth.	We're losing clients, and the chances are we won't be able to keep you on at the end of your training contract.

Recruiting Letters

Every recruiting letter has one of three basic messages: 'Yes', 'Maybe', or 'When hell freezes over'. If you get the last of these, you needn't worry yourself any further. But if the letter says 'Yes' or 'Maybe' you need to read between the lines to know where you really stand. The examples below show you how.

THE YES LETTER
What the firm said:

Waite, Pay, & Pray
1 Midas Avenue
London EC2 A 4JD

Mr Alexander Clarke
Downing College
Cambridge University

31 October 2011

Dear Mr Clarke,

It was a pleasure to meet you last week. You would clearly fit in well with this firm, so on behalf of my partners and myself, I would like to offer you a training contract starting in September 2012.

If you would like to visit our offices and meet some more of our lawyers, do please call my secretary, Lucy Brader, to arrange a mutually convenient time.

I look forward to seeing you again.

Yours sincerely,

Hamish Wilson

What the firm meant:

Waite, Pay, & Pray
1 Midas Avenue
London EC2A4JD

Mr Alexander Clarke
Downing College
Cambridge University

31 October 2011

Dear Mr Clarke,

For someone who started off at an inner-city comprehensive, you've certainly managed to pull yourself up by your bootstraps. Your pale complexion, emaciated physique and overall nerdiness, combined with your consistently brilliant exam results, suggest that you are just the sort of compulsive library-loving swot we're looking for.

No doubt you'll get lots of other offers, because hardcore zealots like you don't grow on trees. Someone so patently willing to sacrifice his health and social life is a real find.

I wouldn't want to introduce you to a client or have a meal with you, but I bet you could rack up enough billable hours in a year to reduce your salary to the equivalent of £3.95 per hour.

I hope we can sign you up.

Yours sincerely,

Hamish Wilson

THE MAYBE LETTER
What the firm said:

Cower, Cringe & Tremble
120 Finsbury Avenue
London EC1 4HB

Ms Georgina Rose
Nelson Hall
University of Westhampton
NH1 2GX

31 October 2011

Dear Ms Rose,

Thank you for coming in to see me last week. I enjoyed our meeting very much. Although I am not able to make you an immediate offer of employment, I know that other partners of the firm would like to meet you for a second interview.

If you are interested in pursuing this invitation, please call our recruitment co-ordinator, Mr Alan O'Flynn, to arrange a mutually convenient time for your visit. You might find it helpful to co-ordinate your visit with interviews at other firms in the City.

Yours sincerely,

Janine Robinson

What the firm meant:

Cower, Cringe & Tremble
120 Finsbury Avenue
London EC1 4HB

Ms Georgina Rose
Nelson Hall
University of Westhampton
NH1 2GX

31 October 2011

Dear Ms Rose,

I was astonished that someone like you — a mediocre student at a second-rate university — would even bother to apply to Cower, Cringe & Tremble. By any standards you're a pitiful specimen.

On the other hand, a bald willingness to ask for something you have no right to is worth a lot in this profession. You couldn't possibly have a real future with us, but we always need more bodies and we can bill your time at the same rates as our decent trainees. Clients can't tell the difference.

I'm not willing to take sole responsibility for hiring you, so you'd better come in and see a few more of our people. Unless you can persuade some other firm to pick up the tab, you're going to have to pay your own way down.

Yours sincerely,

Janine Robinson

Hard Questions

One of the mistakes law students make in interviews is that they sometimes try to be too nice. This is a misconceived strategy, particularly in the law, where deference is seen as a weakness and an ability to fight your own corner is seen as an absolute must. So be prepared to ask some 'hard' questions. You need to know the answers anyway and the interviewers will respect you for asking them.

- How does the firm determine associate's salaries? Are they pegged to 'productivity' (i.e. billed hours)? If so, does the calculation include all the hours spent doing things that associates are frequently asked to do – e.g. pro bono work – but often get no credit for?
- How many associates have left the firm in the past year?
- What kind of training does the firm give its trainees? Is it all 'on the job' training (i.e. nothing)?
- Are any associates presently working on a single big case and if so how long have they been on it? Will *you* be assigned to it?
- Did most (all) of the partners go to public school? How many of them talk with anything other than an Oxford English accent?
- How many hours does the average associate bill each year? (This figure should be lower than the total number of hours in year.)
- Are all trainees automatically offered jobs when they qualify, and do they have a choice as to which department

they join? (Many firms are retaining only 70 per cent of this year's qualifiers.)

- Does the firm have non-equity partners? i.e. 'partners' who are paid a fixed salary rather than a share of the profits. (Non-equity partnership is a sham device for postponing the day of real partnership, in many cases indefinitely.)
- Ask your interviewers – especially the ones you like – if they still expect to be at the firm one year from now. Arriving at a new job to find all the good guys have left for greener pastures is a very unsettling feeling.
- If you fail one of more of your LPC papers, will your firm give you: (a) Time off for retakes on full pay? (b) Time off for retakes without pay? (c) All the time you want for retakes and your P45?

CHAPTER 7

HOW TO SURVIVE (AND MAKE PARTNER) IN YOUR LAW FIRM

*You can make it if you
know what to kiss and whose*

Every day being an associate in a large law firm is like walking a tightrope over shark-infested waters: one wrong step could mean the end. Most associates walk this tightrope with their eyes wide shut.

Survival is the name of the game, and in order to survive in a law firm, it is critical to keep in mind one simple truth: the partners run the show.

Admittedly, some of them run more of it than others, and the idea, which they hold out to the public, that one is accepted as an equal upon attaining the status of a partner is as accurate as saying that South Sudan is the equal of the USA because they're both sovereign states, or that a 1964 E-Type is the same as a Challenger Tank because they both have the same mpg.

The main point from your perspective, however, is that

partners are tenured and you're not. It is hard to get rid of them – and easy to get rid of you. Therefore your goal must be the cultivation of their approval.

Over time this cultivation may become odious to you. As one associate commented: 'They should make my senior partner Pope. That way all I'd have to kiss is his ring.'

Assuming you can stomach the thought of prolonged obsequiousness, how can you ensure that the partners will vote thumbs-up when your name comes up for partnership eight or nine years down the road?

There are two reasons why a partner would vote to bring you into the club: (1) he likes you, and (2) he thinks you'll make him rich.

Practically speaking, he may like you *because* he thinks you'll make him rich – a not uncommon confluence of motivations. Just remember that great warm-nosed dog you had as a child, which nuzzled up to you and wagged its tail when it saw you coming – as long as you continued to feed it.

Try to think of the partners as large furry Labradors with unusually strong appetites.

In order to make the partners like you, you need to make them think you're *like* them, that you're one of them. You even want them to think of you as a surrogate son or daughter (unlike their actual sons and daughters who have revolted against capitalism and sponge off the social security system for a living). Also, in order to make the partners think you'll make them rich, you need to cast yourself in their own preferred self-image: ultra-professional, workaholic and world-beating.

To succeed in this dual quest there are a number of very specific rules that you must follow. These are key maxims that you should tape to your bathroom mirror for review every morning as you tie your tie and trim your nose hairs.

Strict adherence to these rules could, in time, get you a window office, with a secretary who will type one-page letters and deliver phone messages within several days of when they come in. Deviation from them could land you in a basement office across from the post room, sharing a surly secretary whose idea of good service is not chewing her Orbit Sugar-free too loudly when she listens in on your private telephone calls.

Rule 1: Cover Your Arse

This rule is the most important of all the rules, as well as the most difficult to observe. The reason it is difficult to observe is that its command embraces everything you do, no matter how trivial. A discussion of all the applications of this rule could fill several volumes, but some examples will suffice:

Supervise everything your secretary sends out in the post

The stories of letters going out in the wrong envelopes are legion. If your secretary mixes up the memo you intended for your client, in which you point out that his gold bullion sales in Switzerland 'might' have consequences for his capital gains liability, with a letter to the Inland Revenue, saying your client has nothing else to report, you might as well start clearing your desk. This is also true of email. Remember – computers have no secrets. Everything you send out can and will be forwarded to the person you least expect or want to receive it. Whatever you send by email should be suitable for publication on the front page of *The Times*. If it isn't, don't send it out.

This is particularly important when a partner hands you a document and says 'Take a quick look at this and then send it out.' He might very well think it's okay when he gives it to you, but ... in that case why is he giving it to you? What you're seeing is an instinctive effort to cover *his* arse. If a legal argument proves to have been stated inaccurately, or the numbers just don't add up, you can be certain that the next document you proofread will be your CV.

Before sending out any document, clear it with someone – anyone – senior to you
The point is to place responsibility for a mistake anywhere but on yourself. Not only should you run a document past a senior person, but (a) dictate a file memo that you have done so, and (b) somehow let an *even more senior* person know you've cleared the document with the person in-between.

Notify and consult the client about everything you do on his case or project
Clients don't necessarily affect you directly, but remember that they can always have a moan to partners, and in rare instances they will even get upset enough about something to sue the firm.

Your aim should be to build a record – consisting of letters to the client covering *everything* – to make it look as if it is he who is responsible for any disasters that occur.

Partners, you will find, are the ultimate arse-coverers in this way, spending enormous amounts of billable time drafting letters explaining to the client why the firm is doing what it is doing. This could all be done by telephone for one-tenth of the

THE OPEN-DOOR POLICY

'We welcome constructive criticism from trainees and associates'

Law firms love to boast of their openness to criticism and reform. They claim to observe an open-door policy with respect to grievances from trainees and associates, and express an eagerness to hear suggestions from below.

Such claims should be taken with more salt than you'll find in the Dead Sea. Once you get to your firm, try them out. Suggest keeping the heating on during winter weekends because it's difficult to write wearing ski gloves. Ask for soft loo paper – i.e. something less corrosive than computer paper – in the lavatories.

The response from any partner you approach will be 'I'm glad you brought that on up, Sandra. You know, it was a problem when I was an associate. Yes, it's certainly a problem.' This is intended to convey the message: 'I know how you feel. I'm a regular guy.' It also conveys the message: 'I'm not going to do anything about it. No one is. Take it like a man.'

So much for the open-door policy. But why don't associates band together in committees to represent their views on a formal basis to partners. In other words, unionise? Well, they do ... and they don't.

The basic problem is *ambition*. Associates see no long-term benefit in improving their lot, because they don't intend to *be* associates five years down the road. They plan to become part of the management.

The pragmatic way is to take it on the chin, and wait for the day when you're the one dispensing the favours. Until then, hang on to your skiing gloves and your personal roll of Andrex three-ply.

expense, but such a common-sense approach would reduce billings and – even more unacceptable – leave the firm's collective
arse uncovered.

*In reporting meetings or conferences on your time-sheets, factor in
an unknown*
Never just write, 'Attended meeting with Counsel – 1 hour'. Far
too precise. If a partner was there, she might have recorded the
meeting on her time-sheet as lasting only 40 minutes. Even if
you were the only lawyer present, the client might complain to
a partner that he thought the meeting only lasted 40 minutes.
In either case, the discrepancy could be very damaging to your
reputation. You'll never be given the opportunity to prove that
you were the only sober, non-hallucinating, non-schizophrenic
person present. Always say: '*Prepared for and* attended meeting
with Counsel – 1 hour'. Those three extra words, which cost you
nothing, could make all the difference.

The same principle applies when you've spent all day proofreading hundreds of pages of Interest-Rate Swap Agreements. It's not
that you did anything wrong. You were *supposed* to spend all day
proofreading those things. But dress it up a little. Instead of saying
'Proofreading – 9 hours', say, '*Reviewing, editing* and proofreading
– 9 hours'. Again, three little words could make all the difference.

*Before you do any work on a file make sure you understand exactly
what the partner wants*
This is not as easy as it sounds. The partner might want an asser-
tive piece that contains no reference to any authority running
against the client's position. He might want a general survey of
the law, including all authorities whether favourable or unfa-
vourable. He might initially want the latter, but having read
your analysis, decide he wants the former, and wonder why you
didn't give it to him in the first place.

Rarely will he *tell* you what he wants. You've got to try to
second-guess him.

This raises the question of what your immediate response should be when a partner presents you with instructions so garbled that you suspect his sobriety. As a rational person, you will be tempted to ask questions. You will feel an impulse to attempt to clarify the problem and make sure you understand what is required from you.

Resist this impulse! One or two questions are okay, three at most, just to let the partner know you're awake and paying attention as he drones on. (Stifle yawns at all costs.)

But no more. Further enquiry, however reasonable, will only make him nervous about your intelligence and legal acumen. If he hasn't made the problem clear the first time round, it's probably because he doesn't understand it himself.

Your best approach, even in the face of the most wildly confused instructions, is to smile, nod your head, and say 'Yes, I see', 'I understand'. When he has finished (as far as you can tell) leave the office, find a quiet place to vomit and then track down a senior associate to tell you what the hell is going on.

PUT THE BURDEN ON THE CLIENT

When writing to a client to request that he 'verify' and sign an affidavit that you have drafted, don't be too proud to include some weaselly (yet lawyerly) words like the following:

Please read, review, examine, and consider all aspects of this document thoroughly and thoughtfully. Needless to say, you are perfectly, totally, and absolutely free to make any additions, alterations, modifications, corrections, amendments, clarifications, enhancements, breast augmentations, editions, or even changes that you feel are appropriate, necessary, desirable, worthwhile, or good. Thereafter, and only thereafter, if it meets with your full and complete satisfaction, agreement, approval and liking, sign it and…

When you include this sort of material, the *client* is responsible for whatever you've produced, and your arse is covered. (And for God's sake, keep a copy of your correspondence.)

Save all your drafts

It doesn't matter whether you're working on a £10 million oil platform lease, a £2,500 personal injury pleading, or a time-filling memo to put on file. If you show it to a partner (and you should), and he makes you amend it ten or twelve times (and he will), save every version. There's at least a fifty-fifty chance that the partner will call you three days later and say 'By the way, Seager, you did save those early drafts, didn't you?'

This makes no sense whatsoever. If you asked the partner why he wanted them, he would say you never know when some of the material in them might prove useful. But the real reason is that he's scared – not of anything in particular, just scared – like a child at night who insists that his father shine a torch under the bed.

Resist pointing out the absurdity of his request. Humour him. Tell him you've saved every scrap, and they're all just waiting for the time when they might be needed. And make sure they are: you never know when he might show up with a torch to check under the bed.

Make four times as many copies of every document as you can possibly use
This is particularly important for litigation documents, for which you will need:

- an original + copies for filing;
- another copy that the court will 'file stamp' and return to you so that you can prove that you actually filed it;
- 'service copies' for serving on each of the other parties;
- 'intra-office copies'– send one to every lawyer who has ever had anything to do with the case;
- 'client copies' – send one to everyone at the client's offices who you've ever talked to, or who you've heard might be interested in the case;
- your own copy;
- ten copies to replace the other copies that will turn out to have missing pages or that your secretary will have used to clean dog poo off the bottom of her shoe; and
- ten copies just to have around, so you can truthfully answer in the affirmative when a partner asks if you made some extra copies in case of an emergency.

This last point is especially important. If you do not make a ridiculous number of extra copies, the partner in charge will find out and be irritated that you did not make a ridiculous number of extra copies.

Also, and most often overlooked, you should get the client to sign *several* copies of everything you may need to file that requires his signature. The reason is that if the original is lost, someone will have to crawl to the client for a second signature. This is absurd of course, and clued-up clients who recognise arse-covering for what it is will be irritated. There is a better than evens chance, however, that some partner will ask if you had the good sense to take this precaution, and you will need the tangible proof at hand.

Rule 2: Take on as Few Files as Possible

This rule may seem inconsistent with what you've heard about the brutal hours associates are required to work, but it isn't. Yes, you *should* generate some impressive hours, and you should certainly *appear* to be working extremely hard (see Rule 4).

But your goal should be to do an excellent job on a few files, rather than a mediocre job on lots of files, because mediocrity is very out of fashion in law firms. Being a reasonable sort of person you probably think that partners take account of the volume as well as standard of work you're doing, and recognise that there's bound to be a trade-off between the two? Wrong.

First, it's very rare that one partner will know what demands are being placed on you by other partners. They all operate in little black boxes, totally isolated from each other (and often the world). It is fatal to assume that they communicate with each other and that they will not make conflicting demands on your time. They don't. And they will.

Second, even if they did know what other pressures you were under, they wouldn't care. What they care about is the work you do for them. Each one will expect 100 per cent perfection from you on *his* file, and if he doesn't get it, he will (a) resent it, and (b) remember it.

Third, it is a verity that partners have short memories when it comes to an associate's contribution to the firm as a whole. Your overall performance may have been stupendous in view of the number of plates you were spinning at one time, but you can be certain that a few years or even a few months down the road,

REINING IN A PARTNER

A critical skill which every trainee and associate needs to develop is that of preventing the partner with whom they're working from saying something foolish or just plain wrong in front of a client.

Partners tend to bluff a lot in client meetings, and sometimes one of them will go too far. Maybe he doesn't know the area of law as well as he should, or maybe he's just feeling good and gets carried away – anyway, he starts giving advice that you know could send the client into bankruptcy or prison.

Your job in this situation is to stop him. Doing so requires alertness, because you have to see very quickly where the partner is going and cut him off before he reaches the point of no return.

It also requires diplomacy, because you have to intervene without exceeding the limits of your humble station. (You're only there because the partner likes an audience or might want a cup of coffee.)

One approach is to interrupt the partner in mid-sentence: 'Mr Peterson, I can see you're about to make another of your typically brilliant ideas, but perhaps we should first explain to Ms Loram the more conventional approach, so she'll know what her competitors are doing.'

If the outrageous proposal is already on the table, you could say: 'Another way to achieve the same objective – you were explaining this to me only yesterday Mr Peterson – would be to...'

Either of these displays of uncommon boldness on your part will probably startle the partner, like a bucket of cold water, into recognising what he was about to do. At that point he will follow up with: 'Oh, yes. Yes, absolutely. We could do that too. Options, Ms Loram – we want you to know all the options.'

The partner won't love you for doing this and he definitely won't thank you. But don't let the certainty of his ingratitude stop you helping him out. Remember: whenever a partner is made to look stupid in front of a client, it's an associate's head that rolls, not his.

anyone who may once have known the full story will have long since forgotten it.

When partnership evaluation time rolls round, those baggy-eyed months when you foreswore sex and averaged three hours of sleep per night will mysteriously disappear from the collective partnership memory. All they will remember are the plates that you dropped.

This problem of conflicting demands made on associates is hardly of recent vintage. Indeed, having been tackled on it over the years by involuntarily departing associates, partners at most firms are prepared with two facile responses of which you should be aware.

First, they say, associates are expected to act as 'professionals', i.e. to do top-quality work on *everything* they undertake. As a practical matter, this is utterly unresponsive to the problem of conflicting demands on an associate's time. Nevertheless, partners continue to hoist the ill-defined, self-promoting, semi-macho banner of professionalism to support their completely unrealistic expectations.

The second reply partners give is that associates should be mature enough to protect themselves. Take them at their word and CYA (*cover your arse*). Make sure you have a bumper volume of the *Weekly Law Reports* correctly positioned when the boots start flying.

This is easier said than done. The safest and most frequently available approach is to pit the partners against each other, relying on their various levels of seniority to resolve the problem. Thus, when all your available time is being used on a project for Partner Henchley and junior Partner Auld approaches you for help, your response should be no less obsequious and self-protecting than the following:

AULD: You there! I'd like you to help me draft a prospectus for an offer of convertible debentures that Amalgamated Plasterboard plans to put out next month.

YOU: Uh ... that certainly sounds interesting. I enjoy drafting prospectuses and have long been fascinated by the particular issues involved in the plasterboard industry. Can I assume that you have already spoken to Mr Henchley, who said he wanted my full attention devoted to his mother-in-law's will for the next month?

AULD: Henchley, eh? Well, look. Perhaps I can find someone else.

YOU: Oh. Okay. Please let me know if there is any way I can help. I had no plans for this Saturday evening that couldn't be rescheduled for next year.

Note that the only people you can interplead in this manner are partners. Law firms aren't like poker, in which two fives are better than one King. In law, one partner tops four senior associates.

Rule 3: There is No Such Thing as a 'Draft'

In legal circles, some words and expressions have become altered through usage. They take on peculiar meanings, remote from popular understanding. They become what are known as 'terms of art'.

One important term of art is the word 'draft'. Failure to understand its specialised meaning has left many an eager and capable associate consigned to proofreading loan agreements during his (short) stay with the firm.

The potential disaster of misunderstanding the term draft will confront you early in your career: a partner for whom you've been researching an issue asks you to provide her with a 'draft' of a file note on what you've discovered. More often than not she'll camouflage the trap by saying something like 'Just do a draft', or 'Just *whip off* a draft', or even 'Just *dictate* a *rough* draft'. The italicised words should trigger flashing red lights in your mind.

The partner who utters these words does not mean them. When she speaks them, she should be disbelieved. There is no correlation between her expression and her intent.

Notwithstanding how your dictionary might define 'draft' ('a first or preliminary writing, subject to revision'), and regardless of the seven years of Latin and three of Greek that you took, and ignoring the two decades you have spent using the English language in written and spoken correspondence, this partner wants a *polished, final product*.

That she asked for a draft does not mean she will tolerate typos. That she instructed you to produce a 'rough' working document does not mean you should not double-check all the case references in advance. That she said 'dictate' this piece does not mean she will excuse the absence of captions, headings and cross-referenced footnotes.

Everything you submit to a partner should be suitable for framing. No matter how casual the request, how insignificant the task or how small the amount of money at issue, the test you should apply to everything bearing your name is its suitability for hanging in the Sistine Chapel (the *newly restored* Sistine Chapel) of legal documents.

Note an ironic corollary to the rule that there is no such thing as a draft: *everything must be a draft.*

The point is that while everything you submit to a partner must be your best effort, you should never *admit* that it is your best effort. This is because the partner is bound to change it – not because it needs changing, but because changing things needlessly is what partners do.

For this reason you should put the word 'draft' at the top

of everything you submit to a partner, especially things heading ultimately for a client or the court. This conveys two important messages: the first is that it is just a preliminary product, something you could undoubtedly improve upon given a bit more time, the second is that the partner's *invaluable* input will *of course* be necessary to put the document in truly final form.

The first message covers your arse, the second sucks up to the partner – two entirely appropriate messages for someone in your position to be sending.

The communication problem exemplified by partners' continuous misuse of the word draft occurs in a variety of contexts. Take two other notable examples: *'Just skim the case authority'* and *'take a quick look at the case authority in this area'*.

Never should an associate 'skim' anything; and never should an associate take just a 'quick look' at anything. If you miss one case that is even marginally relevant, or one statutory section that is just arguably germane, it will haunt you for years to come.

A last word regarding drafts and other preliminary undertakings: If, in the direst of circumstances, you find yourself unable to complete the exhaustive, perfect work you now know is expected, do not forget Rule 1: CYA.

The best way to do this is to state the limits of your work in a memorandum accompanying what you have produced:

> In the following discussion, I have, as requested, addressed the question of the protection of minority shareholders under S75 of the Companies Act. *I have not addressed the question of directors' duties in connection with such protection.*

The italicised sentence, although spineless, shifts the burden higher up for any catastrophic problems that occur. It suggests, without saying so, that there was an *understanding* that you would limit your research in the way stated.

Other Misleading Expressions

When a partner misuses the word draft, you can protect yourself – if you have read this book and know what he really means.
Often, however, a partner will use a word that signals danger,
but there's absolutely nothing you can do about it – nothing,
that is, short of throwing up on his desk to cut him short.

In some instances this will prove to have been a moderate
response. Below are several of the really serious danger signals
that you should recognise for what they are:

'This project will require some creative thinking'
The partner who approaches you with these words is cunning. He is
about to present you with a problem that he knows has no solution.

Sometimes a client wants to do something he can't do – like
using Lake Windermere as a toxic waste dump. Sometimes
a client *doesn't* want to do something the law says he has to
do – like tell the Inland Revenue about Aunty Dot's surprise
£500,000 bequest.

Whatever the problem, the partner will come to you for
a solution.

It is one of the more craven things a partner will do. He knows
there's no solution, because he's thought about it and couldn't
come up with one – which is what led him to the remark about
creative thinking.

Even if you could come up with a solution, he wouldn't use it,
because the chances are there's no authority for it. If there were
any authority he'd know.

LOATHSOME CLIENTS – DO YOU HAVE TO TAKE ON THE WORK?

Occasionally, you will be asked to help represent someone you don't like. It's not just that the work is tedious and boring (that's to be expected), but that you find the client repugnant for ideological or other reasons. Do you have to take the case?

It depends. Are we talking about a situation in which you just don't like the things your client gets up to even though they're perfectly legal? Tobacco companies for instance who instruct you to prepare a defence against action in tort for nicotine poisoning. If so, the answer is yes, you definitely have to help out on those cases. That's what big firms do. Those kinds of clients are their bread and butter.

But what if it's someone who's done something really awful, something so unspeakably vile that you lose your lunch at the mere thought of the person – Rosemary West, for instance, or Colonel Gaddafi. Do you still have to work on the case?

No. But you don't have to remain employed at your firm either. Turning down work is a risky business.

Actually, there *are* ways you can get out of bad projects. But expressing moral scruples isn't one of them. What you've got to do is tell the partner that you're already busy helping out some *other* odious, repulsive slug stay out of jail. Say: 'Gosh, I'd love to help you on the Vladko Mladic case, Mr Owen, but I'm already up to my eyeballs keeping Karadzic out of trouble.'

Whatever you say, don't attempt to explain your true views to the partner in charge of the gruesome work. He knows people scorn him for what he does, and he's hyper-sensitive to criticism. This is simply no place for candour.

There's a lot of ugly work floating around at the top of the big law firms because the clients who can afford them didn't get that rich by being nice folks. If you don't like occasionally working for the bad guys, you should consider a different job.

This partner is covering his arse. He'd rather you were the one who failed to come up with a solution, in case he has to explain it to a more senior partner or the partner who brought in the client.

If he *is* the partner who brought in the client, he's covering his arse out of habit. After all, that's what got him where he is today.

'Have you ever done any work on [impossibly abstruse and tedious area of law]?'

The partner who asks this question does not care what you answer. If your answer is yes, she'll say, 'Fine, we're going to take advantage of your expertise.' If the answer is no, she will say, 'Fine, you're about to become the firm's expert on this area.'

Her question is almost rhetorical. It is an indirect way of saying you're about to tackle the most mind-numbing area of law known to man. She is justifiably squeamish about telling you this head on, and so tries to disguise it by euphemism.

'Are you busy?'

Your answer to this question should always be an unhesitating 'Very busy', even if you happen to be surfing the web at the time.

Whoever asks you this question is about to ask you to do something – probably something pretty nasty, or they wouldn't have approached you so obliquely. (If the approach is an even more oblique 'How are you fixed for time?' you can be sure the job has four legs and barks.)

If your answer is merely 'Busy', you will be given the job. You may get it even with 'Very busy', but that way you'll at least gain points for carrying a heavy load.

If in fact you're not busy and you think you need the hours, your answer should be the same, but with a qualification (preferably couched in language suggestive of your heroic capacity for toil): 'Very busy, but perhaps I could *shoulder* some more.'

'I'll need about a day's work from you on this file'

This ranks up there with 'We value our trainees', 'Our commercial property department has never been busier' and 'Partnership is guaranteed'.

There is no such thing as a one-day project, at least not one they'd bother getting a new person to do.

'One-day projects' usually involve searches for a case or statutory authority that does not exist. The people in charge have almost certainly checked the obvious sources already and found nothing. Because your search will turn up nothing either, you'll be required to continue it for days on end, wasting incredible amounts of time as you descend the ladder of obscure sources.

'Familiarise yourself with the law in this area'
The partner who says this doesn't mean you should merely find out which statute contains the authority he's looking for. He doesn't mean you should become just roughly conversant with the structure of the legislation in question.

He's using 'familiarise' in the way only partners use it: to *master* an area; to know by heart every clause of every germane statute; to commit to memory every case even vaguely relevant.

It may be that he's just got wind of a deal that's about to happen, or he anticipates a dramatic turn of events in a big case. Whatever he thinks, it'll happen fast, or he wouldn't have given you even the little warning that he did. Moreover, he thinks the area is too complicated to be responsible for it himself. He wants someone else's neck on the line: yours.

Rule 4: Cultivate the Image of a Workhorse
In law, appearance is reality. Rule 4 mandates affirmative

craftiness and cunning. It exhorts you to be resourceful and creative in your quest for the proper image.

To assist you in this quest, below are some life-saving (and marriage-saving) tips on how to maintain the preferred image while keeping your workload under control. These tips fall into five categories:

Judging your Workload

Let's start with a fundamental truth: *Billings are important to your career.* Even at firms that make a great play of being 'full of individuals who value their lives outside the law',* the partners' greatest lament is that there are only twenty-four hours in an associate's day. The fact is that, whatever law firm you go to, some level of work is unavoidable. But what level?

The answer to this question depends on your peers at the firm. For appearance's sake, you're going to have to spend roughly as much time working as they do.

But only *roughly* as much. This brings us to one of the major tips to ease your burden: do not so much as *think* about trying to lead the field in billable hours.

Not even if the field consists of you and old Mrs Walters in residential conveyancing.

For one thing, you won't be able to do it. There are always a few superhuman grinds around.

More importantly, that's not how you want to spend your life. You want more on your tombstone than 'Andrew Palmer, Partner'. You'd like to have at least enough free time to be able to show up for your own divorce.

The only goal you should set for yourself is to avoid the anchor position in your year. That's good enough. For once in your life, as contrary as it is to your nature, be average.

---

* What these firms are full of is something quite different, and much better for plant growth.

Easy Hours: How to Beef up your Billings Legitimately
Given that you're going to have to chalk up some hours, you should take every possible advantage of the few easy but legitimate ways of beefing up your billings.

Most of your work will not be easy. It might consist of researching safety requirements for offshore oil rigs, drafting motions for enlargement of time (only a lawyer would attempt to 'enlarge' time), or doing a comparative study of Clean Air Regulations in the UK, France and Sweden.

Such work is boring (you will find yourself filling out time-sheets for fun) and extremely tedious. It is analogous to digging ditches in a minefield, which doesn't take much intelligence, isn't glamorous or remotely enjoyable, but you do need to pay close attention to what you're doing.

When something easy comes your way, pounce on it. Of the various but legitimate ways to beef up your billable hours, at least three will be available no matter where you work:

Travel
The first and best of these is travel. A shrewd associate will involve himself in work for continental clients, preferably corporate work that will entail trips to the company's headquarters. The time spent en route to Paris, Milan or Barcelona is billable, and it is a gift from God from your point of view. Okay, you *might* have to spend the flight reviewing client papers. On the other hand, you might have to order a double Scotch and watch *The Bourne Ultimatum.*

Court Work
The second source of easy hours involves court work of any kind. By the time a case actually reaches court, the solicitor's role is practically over. Your client's barrister takes over and you can sit back and pay only the vaguest attention to what is going on.

To make your client feel secure (you're there in a sort of hand-holding capacity) and to prevent yourself falling asleep, you should pass little notes to Counsel every now and then. It doesn't really matter what they say, as merely passing them will convince your client that you're on top of the situation.

You should also bring along a suitcase full of blue ruled notebooks. Unless there is someone more junior on your team, you may get lumbered with the job of noting down every single word uttered in court, but that needn't disturb your reverie: you've had many years of practice of noting without listening at law school. Old skills like that are easily recalled.

Proofreading

Finally, there are easy hours to be had in proofreading. Every written item that leaves the firm has to be proofread. The partners expect it to be done, and the clients expect, however grudgingly, to pay for it.

You don't want to find yourself proofreading too often: it looks silly on your CV as your primary field of expertise. Still, it has the primary virtue of being something you can do at home, stretched out on your sofa, eating Kettle Chips and listening to your iPod. Also, noticing a few typos that everyone else has missed (a 'catch' in legal parlance – as in 'Nice catch, Dave. I didn't see that one') can earn big points in the eyes of the partner overseeing the project.

GETTING AWAY FROM IT ALL

Projects that get you out of the office are not to be taken for granted. Better still are those projects which not only get you out of the office, but get you somewhere where it doesn't matter how you're dressed. (Projects where it doesn't matter *if* you're dressed are few and far between.)

Even if this means trekking off to some God-forsaken plot of land to serve an eviction order on 'travellers' who have taken a shine to it or spending two days in a client's basement rummaging through boxes of VAT records, you will come to relish the opportunity to shed your suit (which hasn't been to the dry cleaners in 18 months), your absurd tie (whose only function is to collect tangible memories of your meals) or your uncomfortable tights (which only make it difficult to go to the loo).

Note: if you're wearing the absurd tie *and* the uncomfortable tights, being stuck in the office isn't your primary problem.

Weekend Work: Avoiding it, Simulating it

A legal career inevitably involves some weekend work. It was a lawyer who said 'Thank God it's Friday – only two more working days till Monday.'

A question confronting all associates is how to know when weekend work is really necessary. Legal work is like schoolwork, in that you could *always* do more in any given area (or like psychoanalysis, in that the more you get into it the uglier things look).

Your goal, of course, is to minimise weekend work. Free weekends are what it's all about.

To keep your Saturdays and Sundays as free as possible, bear in mind that weekend work is of two types. First, there is serious big-time work that has been brewing for some time. It could be a major complaint to the Competition Commission that you've been involved in, the papers are due by Monday morning, and you are regrettably the logical person to spend the necessary weekend time buffing up the brief.

FRIDAY AFTERNOON – THE ART OF LAYING LOW

Friday afternoon is a critical time. It's the time when partners start checking their diaries to see what needs to be filed in Court on Monday morning. It's the time when your weekend stands the greatest chance of being destroyed.

Try to avoid answering your phone after Friday midday. On no account should you check with your secretary for messages. Once you've been told that some partner was looking for you, you're stuck. (After the way you've treated your secretary, she certainly cannot be trusted to hide the fact that you don't return your Friday afternoon calls.)

Avoid walking past partners' offices on the way to the lavatory. If possible, don't even go to the lavatory on Friday afternoon. If you absolutely have to, find a nice end-of-row cubicle and stay there for the rest of the day.

Ideally, you should arrange to be out of the office altogether. An appointment with your dentist will do. If that isn't possible, the next best strategy is to set up camp in a corner of the library. Take your books and files and whatever you're working on with you – the bigger the pile you surround yourself with, the better. You want to give an impression of utter immovability.

Make sure it's an *obscure* corner of the library. It's not unusual for partners to actually prowl around on Friday afternoons in search of hapless associates for weekend duty.

Of course, it is impossible to turn off your Blackberry for long, and the days when associates could genuinely hide from prowling partners are long gone. Email and text messaging have made every associate's life that much less bearable, and as mobile phone coverage gets more uniform and reliable, that old favourite excuse – 'sorry, there's no reception in Fulham' – gets that much less believable.

There is no escape from such work. You should resign your-self to it, exploiting the opportunities it will afford to enhance your image as a hard worker. If the partner in charge takes the extraordinary step of *asking* whether you will be able to help out over the weekend, and you have sized up the situation and seen that you are the obvious choice for the job, tell her you'll defi-nitely be coming in.

Moreover, pretend you're glad about it. Tell her you were planning to be in the office anyway. Tell her you *like* weekend work, because it gives you a chance to hunker down without lots of interruptions from the telephones. (Don't worry about the credibility of such an absurd claim: lots of partners really do like weekends for this very reason.)

Above all, do not make her order you to be there. She'll do it, so you won't have gained anything, but she won't like doing it. Once you've started rubbing her conscience the wrong way or convinced her that you're not a team player, you might as well pack your bags and move on.

The other type of weekend work is emergency work: short-term, last-minute, run-of-the-mill stuff that any associate could do. This type of work you can avoid.

This isn't your emergency; it isn't something they need *you* to handle. In all probability, some partner hasn't bothered taking care of a matter that has been lying around for ages, because he knew there was a stable of associates he could get to deal with it at the last minute.

Any associate can deal with these types of emergencies, and you shouldn't be concerned about the propriety of trying to avoid them. What you should be concerned about is *how* to avoid them. It can be done. (See *Friday Afternoons*, above.)

You might well wonder about the costs of such an approach. Won't people get angry if you consistently manage to avoid weekend work? It's unlikely they'll ever know. No one keeps a checklist of weekends worked. Still, it's worth covering your arse here, as everywhere. There are a number of handy devices for doing this.

Back in the good old days, before mobile phones and Blackberries spoiled everything, the following ruse worked wonders: since many firms had a receptionist coming in for all or part of each Saturday, the wily associate could create an excellent opportunity. Whether he intended to lounge about all day watching telly, playing golf, or getting some horizontal recreation on Saturday morning, he would set the alarm for about eleven, call the office, and (using a false voice) have himself paged.

Everyone who was really at the office would assume that he was there too, somewhere. That they didn't see him did not matter: law firms are big places. And it didn't even matter that the receptionist would know he hadn't answered his paging call. Lots of people didn't – as a matter of principle. (The well-known principle of being difficult and tiresome for the sake of it.)

But in this era of instant communications the office pager has gone the way of carbon paper, and such halcyon days are long gone. Nowadays the only device for simulating weekend work at work is much more demanding. It involves actually going in.

This doesn't have to ruin your plans for the weekend. You don't have to *stay* there. Just go in, look a bit fatigued (not totally knackered – you're supposed to be able to take the pressure), walk briskly through the library, grab two or three volumes of law reports, return to your office, turn on the lights, and then head for the first tee. (Don't worry about the fact that you can get the law reports online – plenty of partners are technophobic and still like the warm feel of bound leather reports.)

Turning on your lights is important. The cleaners will have turned them all off on Friday night, so anyone who sees yours burning brightly will assume you've been in.

The joy of this trick is that it keeps working all weekend. In many office buildings, the cleaners won't be round again till Monday evening, so you get the benefit all day Saturday, all day Sunday and even early Monday morning.

UNDERSTANDING BILLABLE HOURS

When lawyers talk about billable hours, they usually refer to annual figures. Below is a chart that breaks down the annual figures into weekly figures and then puts them into perspective.

In evaluating these figures, bear in mind that billable hours don't (or *shouldn't*) include time you spend eating lunch, arranging a game of squash, or discussing last week's episode of *Beverly Hills 90210*. An accepted rule of thumb is that forty billable hours requires sixty hours in the office (except in some City practices where you start billing as soon as you wake up).

Annual Total	Weekly Average	Interpretation
4,000	80	Wrong profession; junior doctor.
3,500	70	Pathological liar.
3,000	60	Barely conceivable, and then only if living with camp bed in office.
2,500	50	Sweatshop hours. Brutal but possible, given lots of travel. Probably guilty of substantial padding.
2,000	40	Very respectable in most practices.
1,500	30	Civilised lifestyle, assuming no heavy non-billable duties.
1,000	20	An associate with this number could only survive if he calls the Senior Partner 'Dad'.
500	10	Sole practitioner (Tiverton).
25	0.5	Dead (but no one has realised it yet).

Turning your light on after the cleaners have been is a trick capable of application during the week too. If they do their rounds past your office at, say, seven o'clock, and you happen to finish your game of squash at 7.15, just pop back and turn on your angle poise lamp. It can't hurt your image with the partners who pass by later that night or the few who come in early next day.

If you do come in on a weekend, consider leaving a note on the desk of a partner, just to let her know you were in. You have to be careful with this ruse, because it can be a bit transparent. Don't do it *every* weekend, and don't write in red ink at the top of the note 'Saturday, 7.00 p.m.' Let the partner work out when the note must have been written by, for instance, observing that it was written on the back of that weekend's Church Service programme. (How you get one of those without having to sit through a thirty-minute sermon is another matter.)

The third method of simulating weekend work requires you to ingratiate yourself with the security guard stationed at the office on weekends. With flattery and perhaps a bottle of The Famous Grouse, you might be able to persuade him to sign your name on the check-in list that a lot of law firms maintain on weekends.

All those who actually come in will see your name as they sign their own. Even better, they *won't* see a mark beside your name indicating that you've left – clear evidence that you've outlasted them all.

The only danger with this trick is that others may be doing the same thing. If fifteen associates' names appear in alphabetical order in identical handwriting, someone may sense a sham.

All-Nighters

All-night work has much in common with weekend work. It's unpleasant and should be minimised, but it gives you an opportunity to enhance your image as a hard worker.

Like death, all-nighters cannot be avoided indefinitely. When your number comes up, remember two points: (a) do it gracefully; and (b) don't keep it a secret.

The first point is of primary importance. Because everyone has to do an all-nighter at some time, no one is going to feel sorry for you. If you whine about it, you won't even get credit for your dedication, because everyone will know you did it grudgingly.

The preferred posture is one of ease and nonchalance. This suggests that you are possessed of unusual stamina. (Let your colleagues think that you wouldn't *ever* go to bed but for social reasons.)

It also suggests that you do this sort of thing all the time, which carries the further implication that other, more senior lawyers view you as the person to call upon in a crisis – the can-do guy. Over time it will have partners and associates alike believing that you get called in for the *hard* cases.

The only problem is that your 007-like insouciance under pressure will be wasted if no one knows about it. Hence the second point: don't keep your all-nighter a secret.

In practice this point can conflict with the goal of handling the all-nighter gracefully. Talking about it incessantly is inconsistent with shrugging it off as commonplace. Thus, you should make considerable efforts not to do all-nighters by yourself. With someone else present, word of your energy and stamina will spread.

If you can't arrange company, don't despair. You can make your exertions known to the partner in charge of the case by showing up in his office next day wearing the same clothes as the day before.

When doing this, make sure your clothes are orderly (shirt tucked in, belt buckled, bra facing forwards), because you don't want to look out of control. However, your shirt should be wrinkled, and your beard shadow suitably dark (particularly impressive on women) – these things you couldn't be expected to do anything about.

Another reason you shouldn't be too distressed by a lack of company for your all-nighter is that when you're alone you can take naps on the conference room sofa. Before lying down, however, set your phone to wake you up early the next morning. It's professionally embarrassing to be caught bashing out Zs when you're supposed to be polishing up a flotation document.

General Image Tips

Keep your secretary busy. This is especially important if you share a secretary with a partner. The partner will gauge your productivity from the amount of work you give your secretary.

Not that any of it will actually get done. The secretary will use the partner's work as a pretext for avoiding yours so she can finish the latest issue of *Heat*. She isn't there to *work* eight hours a day – at least not for some lowlife associate.

Nevertheless, you must make the effort.

One way to give the impression that you are keeping your secretary busy is to keep her in-tray loaded with documents. What kind of documents doesn't matter. If you need one letter copied, attach that letter to two or three large files and leave the whole stack in her box. The partner will see the stack and be impressed (of course, you could email it to her, but stacks of paper documents are so much more impressive).

Some particularly important image tips relate to those occasions when you want to knock off a little early – say, around lunchtime.

This will occur once in a while – hey, you've got a life to lead. But cover your arse. This is much more difficult than it used to be – the now-ubiquitous Blackberry has made the oppressed associate's life so much more difficult.

If you must slip out early, always leave by the stairs rather than the lift. Even if you're on the 10th floor. A partner who sees you heading for the ground floor in a lift will be suspicious, no matter how full your briefcase or how purposeful your expression. On the stairs you can speed up or slow your pace to avoid

SIGNS OF LIFE

1.   Light burning brightly.

2.   Suit jacket on back of chair.

3.   Uncapped pen.

4.   Computer turned on and logged in (turn off your screen saver permanently).

5.   Full cup of coffee. (Make sure it's full; half cups are common.)

6.   Half-eaten sandwich.

7.   Phone with blinking 'hold' button.

8.   Open *Weekly Law Reports*.

9.   Shoes. (How far could you have gone without your shoes?)

10. Open briefcase. (Keep a spare around for this purpose. You should be carrying your first one when you leave the office.)

11. Open filing cabinet. (Partners could never believe you'd leave it open all night.)

12. Legal pad with writing cut off in mid paragraph, or even mid-sen...

Signs of Life

meeting anybody else and, in extremis, you can always duck into the lavatories located next to the stairwell.

Secondly, prepare for any telephone calls that might come in after you've gone. You don't want your secretary telling partners that she doesn't know where you are, but she saw you leaving at midday carrying your golf clubs and wearing your designer shades. Partners take a dim view of associates who work a half-day (or a quarter-day, as it would be for some City firms.)

Tell your secretary or the receptionist – whoever will get your calls in your absence – that you're off to a meeting (you don't need to say *which* meeting.) Say you'll be back when it's finished, but it might not end until well after close of business. The point you want to convey is that although she might not see you again till tomorrow, she should tell callers that you've gone 'out', not 'home'.

If you're worried that a partner who gets this message might work late that night and wonder why he didn't see you around, call in for messages after nine holes. Otherwise just be prepared to say that, because of where the meeting was held, it made more sense to stay there to finish reviewing 'the documents' (there are always documents) than to return to the office.

What about partners who pass your office in the early evening and see no signs of life? Make sure there *are* signs of life.

Your light should be on, of course. That's basic.

But go the extra mile. Leave a suit jacket in plain view, preferably on the back of your chair. Shrewd associates keep a spare jacket in the office specifically for this purpose. (Make sure it's the *jacket* you leave rather than your trousers. The implications are entirely different.)

Also, leave a full cup of coffee on your desk. Lawyers make a lot of money, but most of them are tighter than a camel's bum in a sand-storm. They just can't believe someone would waste a *whole* cup of coffee.

In your quest for the image of a workhorse, keep in mind that you can score big points by being in the right place at the right time. If the firm has a partnership meeting at 7.30 a.m. on the first Wednesday of every month, find some excuse for strolling by the meeting room at 7.25 a.m. with your sleeves rolled up and your hair *not* bearing that just-got-out-of-bed' look.

The same principle applies on days when either the weather or Bob Crowe's RMT has yet again brought the public transport system to a halt. Half the secretaries will call in swearing that their cars won't start. You might be tempted to do the same. But in these situations you have a tremendous opportunity to amass huge brownie points.

Set your alarm for what will seem like the middle of the night, and make an all-out effort to get to the office by seven. Invariably, one or two partners will have done the same thing, motivated by white-collar machismo to be able to tell their friends the strike didn't keep *them* from the office.

When they see you there early, they will recognise you as 'their kind of guy'. They won't commend you – you're only doing what you're expected to do. But they'll remember it and always think better of you than your lightweight work-shy colleagues who weakened when the going got tough. An example of the degree of dedication you should simulate was provided by the bombing of St Mary Axe in April 1992 which blew out 300 windows of Norton Rose's offices. According to their marketing manager 'One partner was thrown right across his office by the force of the blast. He went straight back to his desk and carried on working.' Mad? No, just dedicated.

A final tip on cultivating the proper image: never leave your office without a volume of law reports or pad of legal paper tucked under your arm. Even if you're just taking a leak. Keep a biro in your hand, or better still a fountain pen without its top – implying that any pause you take in your heroic travail is going to be so brief that the nib won't have a chance to dry.

Over the years, partners will subconsciously come to associate you with the implements of labour. That association will help carry you where you want to go.

Rule 5: Avoid Peripheral Involvement in Anything

Every now and then, you will be called on to perform a small task in connection with a big case. The partner in charge will assure you that your time commitment will be minimal and that your end of the work will be both interesting and educational.

Use any excuse to avoid this task. It can only bring misery.

Your work will not be interesting. No case is so interesting that it cannot be broken down into boring constituent pieces, and the premise of your involvement is that you will be working on one of the most subordinate pieces.

Nor will your work be educational. No one will explain the background of the case to you or bother to keep you informed of its progress. You will work in an absolute void – not dissimilar from what your social life has become since you joined the firm.

That the work will be boring and educationally worthless is the least of your problems. *Lots* of your work will be boring and educationally worthless.

The main problem is the enormous potential for damage to your reputation. Once you have done anything on a case, people expect you to know everything there is to know about it, and they'll think you're a complete imbecile if you don't have every one of its details at your fingertips.

LAVATORY ETIQUETTE

Partners don't like seeing associates in the lavatory. It means they aren't in their offices racking up the hours. Your objective should be to meet partners in there so rarely that they start looking for the outline of your colostomy bag under your suit jacket.

Never follow a partner into the lavatory. If you go in and see one already there, do a sharp about-turn and leave. If you're already installed in a cubicle when a partner comes in, take the precaution of lifting your legs off the ground so that your shoes and trouser bottoms are no longer visible from the other side of the cubicle door. Some partners have developed the skill of identifying work-shy associates just by the pattern of their soles. Wait until he goes into a cubicle himself and, as far as you can tell, has committed himself to being there. Then make your escape.

If you're standing at the urinal when a partner comes in, simply close up shop and leave. This is no great hardship; most associates can't function with a partner nearby anyway. (If the partner occupies the urinal right next to you, even though there are ten empty ones in the room, you face an entirely different set of issues.)

It is a truism of big-firm life that entering the lavatory causes your Blackberry to ring immediately. Conspiracy theorists allege that the lavatory seats are equipped with heat-seeking sensing devices and that each associate's buttocks are individually coded into the system. Partners at firms we spoke to would neither confirm nor deny this allegation.

If you're determined to take something to read with you, make it a letter or something that will fit into your pocket. Don't stop at Reception, tuck *The Times* under your arm, and head on in. So brazen a declaration of your plans for the next fifteen minutes is crass in the extreme.

The combination of stress, coffee, egg and bacon sarnies, and legal documents gives the average lawyer the natural gas output of New Zealand. Releasing this in your office mysteriously summons your secretary. Unlike your university colleagues, she will not think this hilarious. Neither will you when the work stops getting done.

They forget the tangential nature of your involvement and become irritated by your lack of comprehension. The fact that you don't know what is going on is not mitigated in their eyes by the fact that no one has *told* you what is going on.

To add insult to injury, you will forever after be on called on for emergencies requiring weekend work and all-nighters in connection with the case. In big cases, emergencies occur all the time, and an associate who has done as little as fifteen minutes of work on such a case is deemed to have special responsibilities with respect to its most onerous tasks.

This problem of peripheral involvement is not unlike that of becoming familiar with an objectionable area of law. Once you have so much as glimpsed the Industrial Waste (River Protection) Act you are forever deemed to be the firm's expert on the subject.

The lesson? Where possible avoid any cases that strike you as odious, regardless of how minimal your involvement is likely to be. And remember: your willingness to play the role of the courteous dinner guest, cheerfully consuming whatever slop is put in front of you, will only bring you second, third and fourth helpings of the same.

Rule 6: Give Partners What They Want

Lawyers like to think of themselves as scholars. It's the way they explain to themselves why they don't earn as much as investment bankers.

But if you want to succeed in a large firm, shed all pretensions of scholarship. Practising law is a trade. Notwithstanding what you learned in law school, a lawyer is like a garage mechanic, except that the lawyer charges more because his toolbox is made of leather and called a 'briefcase'.

What partners want from you when they ask for a summary of some point of law is something they can insert wholesale into an opinion letter.

This doesn't mean your product should be clear and readable. You *are* a lawyer.

But it should not be an article for publication in a Sweet & Maxwell periodical. If you produce a think-piece, or an academic treatise, they'll make you do it again.

No doubt this will frustrate you. Throughout law school the professors emphasised the scholarly aspects of law. You learned that following an argument to its impossible but logical conclusion is where it's at.

Ignore all that. Satisfying clients is what the partners are trying to do. Satisfying partners is what you're trying to do.

Rule 7: Stay Alert to Your Long-Term Prospects
If you are content at your law firm and doing well, there is no reason you should not stick around indefinitely. On the other hand, if you expect to leave the firm, whether voluntarily or with a size ten footprint on your rear end, you should know that a junior associate enjoys greater mobility than a senior one.

DIPPING YOUR PEN IN THE COMPANY INKWELL

The traditional taboo on intra-office intimacies — 'don't dip your pen in the company inkwell' — has been expressed in a number of different ways. Most notable is the 'hamburger rule', which advises against getting your meat at the same place you get your bread.

Every firm has at least one lecherous partner. More often than not, this person is male. Lecherous female partners are not common features of the legal landscape — the profession is not so advanced.

This lecher may or may not be single. He may or may not be attractive. He is, invariably, smooth and confident. He will sit down in your office, cross his legs, and straighten his tie in a slick way that says here, at last, is a guy who really knows how to sit down, cross his legs and straighten his tie.

What you should realise, if you find yourself attracted by this act, is that in the end you will be just another notch on his bedpost. He may come on subtly: 'Amazing, your eyes are the same blue as my Ferrari.' Or he may be more direct: 'How about lunch on Sunday? Come round early ... say, Saturday night.' However the liaison begins, it won't last. Afterwards, you'll just be another source of office smirks.

Don't even imagine that having a fling with a partner will advance your career. Certainly, *he* may become an ally in your fight for advancement (though even that is doubtful), but you'll make enemies of all the other partners, who will be green to the gills that one of their colleagues is having more fun than they are.

As far as 'horizontal integration' is concerned (i.e. associates getting friendly with other associates) the dangers are fewer. Your motives are not suspect, because the alliance cannot enhance your competitive position.

The major problem in going out with another associate is, of course, what happens after you break up. Unless your firm is gigantic, you will still bump into each other on a regular basis. You will have to suffer in silence when he or she turns up at the Christmas party with a new companion. (Groin kicks are considered unprofessional except in certain West End firms.)

Perhaps the best policy with respect to intra-office affairs is to apply a 'rebuttable presumption against' i.e. it is presumed that the costs will always outweigh the benefits, but the presumption may be rebutted in exceptional cases. For women, such special cases have been called the 'Brad Pitt Exception'. For men, the 'Gisele Bundchen Principle'. In these cases, the costs of an affair *can't* outweigh the benefits.

Law firms prefer legal virgins, so to speak. They think that a lawyer who has spent more than a few years elsewhere has lost something vital.

It's also a question of inter-firm competition and pride. Firms are hypersensitive to the suggestion that they might be willing to take on an associate who didn't cut the mustard elsewhere. Some of the most prestigious firms are the most insecure in this respect, snubbing 'used' associates like so much dental floss.

Finally, a young associate has greater credibility than one who is, say, five years qualified, when he claims that the first firm just didn't live up to his expectations – that it didn't, for example, have enough work to keep people busy past eight or nine o'clock at night ('and I just couldn't stay at a place where they work part-time').

Law firm recruiters reinforce the theory of immobility between firms by telling you that you'll never have a second chance to join their firm if you don't join them now. 'Turn us down now', they'll imply, 'and that's it.'

In reality the doors to the Church are always open. Okay, perhaps not *always* open, or not at *every* church. And you might have to give up a year or so in seniority in transition, but you're certainly not trapped for life.

Remember, it's a lot easier to switch firms than switch spouses – and people do both all the time.

If the problem at a given firm is that *you* don't like *it*, you needn't worry too much about how it regards you. You don't want to make such a hash of things that they padlock your office and give a pack of rabid Dobermanns a whiff of your handkerchief. But basically, you are the one that decides when to walk.

If, on the other hand, you are happy where you are and could imagine still being there five or ten years down the road, you need to keep a look-out for the various indicators of your progress compared to your peers.

There is really only one indicator that matters, although it travels under many names: bread, dosh, dough, cash, wodge, readies – some have even been heard to call it 'money'.

You will hear stories of other indicators, such as interesting work, travel, nice office space, or a secretary willing to correct typos. The firms themselves will tell you that your annual performance appraisal is the best way of telling how you're doing, although no associate in his right mind believes that (except in negative circumstances where, for instance, the evaluating partner demands your office key and asks where you would like your post forwarded to).

But if money isn't everything, it is definitely way ahead of whatever comes second. If you fall behind the rest of your year in salary, you would be well advised to start buffing up your CV.

The Star System

Law firms operate on a star system. By the time of qualification, a few associates will already have been identified as the stars of their year. There's no formal awards ceremony, but everyone knows who they are.

Being singled out as a star is a self-fulfilling prophecy. Stars receive the best work (such as it is) and the most responsibility – in short, the greatest opportunities to shine.

You don't get to be a star by caring about the outside world. If you've already been designated a star, you aren't reading this book.

The big question is: what if you're not one of the stars of your year. Do you bail out? Work three times as hard? Sabotage the stars?

If you're sure that being a star is what you really want, hang in there a year or two. The fact that you're not a star yet doesn't mean that all the vacancies are permanently filled. Circumstances can cause a star's lustre to fade.

On *Not* Making Partner

Even with the help of this book, there's a chance you won't make partner. Most associates don't.

Times are hard for law firms these days, and partners are looking for reasons *not* to let you on board, rather than the reverse.

Make no mistake: doing excellent work is no guarantee of partnership. Often the partners just don't feel like dividing the cake any farther. And why should they? *Lots* of associates do excellent work. The legal profession is blessed – and cursed – with a surplus of talent.

Partnership decisions are said to reflect the Screwee Rule:

6 SIGNS THAT YOU'RE ON THE WAY OUT

How can you tell when things aren't going well for you, that the partners consider you an 'also-ran', that you're on your way out?

The subtlest of bad tidings is being fed poor quality work. Instead of growing less boring and tedious over the years, your files continue to extend new semantic reach to those two adjectives. However, given that all associate work is boring and tedious, it can be hard to discern a trend one way or the other. (It's like asking whether French lorry drivers are more objectionable than French farmers — it's just impossible to say.)

A somewhat clearer sign is being 'frozen out' altogether: new work just isn't sent your way. At first this seems like a blessing — you're exhilarated to have your evenings free, and you revel in being able to spend ten minutes in the sunshine at lunch. Then you realise your learning curve is plummeting, you find it difficult to get into three figures on your weekly time-sheet, and you begin to dread going into the office because of the whispers that accompany your every step.

Take heart. Don't sit in doubt, wondering when the axe is going to fall. Watch out for the signs below, and you'll be able to predict with complete accuracy the moment of truth:

1. Your new office has no desk, no window and a seat that flushes.
2. The librarian asks for collateral each time you take out a book.
3. Your annual salary rise is in four figures — including the ones to the right of the decimal point.
4. The firm formally considers you for partnership every three months, just so they can tell you you've been passed over *again*.
5. You're given work from people junior to yourself — including the post room.
6. Your client contact is restricted to clients whose wills have become effective.

they'll do it to you if they can. The only associates they can't afford to screw are those who've either developed their own clients – Young Rainmakers – or shrewdly carved out indispensable areas of expertise.

If you get shot down, ask yourself if life would have been so marvellous even if you'd made it Are those really the people you wanted to spend the rest of your life with? Not making partner could be compared to getting bounced out of a leper colony: the world outside may be better than the one you're leaving.

...and the Consequences

What exactly happens if you don't make partner? You die – usually in poverty, always in disgrace. Most spurned associates leave their firm within weeks; others last a few months – long enough anyway to see their spouse commence divorce proceedings.

The most common cause of death is starvation, although a surprising percentage are able to overcome the immobilising effects of depression sufficiently to take their own lives.

A few find positions delivering take-away pizzas – but they too invariably lose the will to live once the other moped riders find out what happened and begin mocking them.

In any event death seems merciful after a few weeks of the indignities that befall passed-over associates. Some of the least of these indignities are:

- Your children come home from school every day with bloody noses and bruises, after fighting with other children chanting, 'Oliver's father wasn't made a *paaartnerrr*.'
- Your children stop coming home from school with bloody noses and bruises because they've begun claiming they were adopted.
- Strange dogs approach you and pee on your leg.
- Strange people approach you and pee on your leg.
- You pee on your own leg.

12 WAYS TO END A LEGAL CAREER

1. When one of the partners announces that his wife is pregnant, distribute a memo denying responsibility.

2. On the morning of a big court case, tell the partner in charge that it's a shame that Match of the Day was such a cliff-hanger last night, because you would have liked to have time to check your case authority properly.

3. Come into the office at the crack of noon — two days in a row.

4. Tell a client how the time he's been billed for was really spent.

5. Send polemical letters to *The Times* on the firm's notepaper and signed in the firm's name.

6. At the Christmas party, get drunk and vomit on the Senior Partner's wife.

7. Voice your opinion that internal procedures described in John Grisham's *The Firm* bear an uncanny resemblance to those of your own firm.

8. Score with a secretary that a partner has been stalking for months.

9. After a game of squash one lunchtime, hang your jockstrap or bra (or both) on a conference room door handle to dry.

10. Suggest that conflicts of interest preclude your firm from acting for Proctor & Gamble.

11. Fail to read this book.

12. Write this book.

14 PRACTICAL SKILLS THEY OUGHT TO OFFER VETERAN LAWYERS – *BUT DON'T*

1. Not talking about law on social occasions.
2. Resisting the call of nature during contract negotiations.
3. Making bills look reasonable.
4. Pretending the associates who work for you may make partner one day.
5. Persuading rich people you're a fantastic lawyer.
6. Persuading friends and relatives you're a hopeless lawyer.
7. Sucking up to secretaries and other support staff.
8. Pretending you respect your partners.
9. Pretending you trust your partners.
10. Pretending you like your partners.
11. Pretending you like your partners' spouses.
12. Pretending you've never fooled around with your partners' spouses.
13. Reconciling the demands of work and getting divorced.
14. Retiring before you're pushed out by your partners.

CHAPTER 8

ONCE YOU'RE A PARTNER

The end of the rainbow

A legal career could be viewed as a kind of journey – but to where? Questioning the destination may be pointless if you're convinced you've gone as far as you're going to, but for those of you who feel you're still en route, who dare to hope for something more, maybe it's not too late.

The mere thought of partnership mesmerises some associates. They daydream about it, drooling unconsciously like a Basset Hound contemplating an old marrow bone, or a trusts-and-estates lawyer contemplating an old marrow bone (for pretty much the same reasons).

According to associate myth, partnership is a blissful state, synonymous with heaven, paradise, nirvana and other realms free of famine, disease, war and proofreading.

If you subscribe to this view, stop and think for a moment. Ask yourself why partners continue to leave their office lights on when they go home at night. Who are they trying to impress?

Ask yourself why they still make a big show of reading

documents while they're standing at the urinals; why you never see a partner idling round the coffee machine chatting about last night's telly with the secretaries. Whose approval are they trying to cultivate?

Is something amiss in paradise?

Whether partnership will even approach your fantasies depends on a number of factors, most importantly the size of your firm.

The most obvious difference between large and small firms is size. Hence the labels 'large' and 'small'.

But the differences don't stop there.

The Small Firm

At a small firm, making partner might bring only a marginal improvement to your working life. Consider four key criteria:

Grunt Work

At small firms, staffing is, by definition, lean. This means there are limits on how much grunt work you can avoid.

Okay, you won't have to do as much as before, but you'll have to do *some* – definitely more than enough to keep you from forgetting, when all is said and done, that you're still practising the same law you did as an associate.

Money

Small firms aren't supported by a proletariat of associates who generate three times as much in client fees as they're paid. You don't get a gush of money to the pyramid's apex the way you do in large firms, because the pyramid's the size of a small chunk of Toblerone.

This means that unless you're a recognised specialist with enough clout to play ball with the big-league firms, the only yacht you'll be sailing when you make partner at a small firm is the kind with a rubber band motor that you still play with in the bath.

Job Security

Job security in the law is dependent on clients like BP and Glaxo which need millions of pounds worth of legal work, year in, year out. Even in a recession, they're a *fantastic* gravy train – but only the big firms can climb aboard. Kevin Dink in the Mile End Road may be every bit the litigator that Sir George Campbell of Broadgate Towers is, but if he pitches for BP's account the only thing he'll win is top marks for chutzpah.

The other disadvantage small firms face is the constant and calamitous possibility of a partnership split. What do you do if your sole expert on the 'One-Bite' Rule leaves to set up his own dog-law boutique?

Prestige

How great can the prestige at a small firm be? You can't impress people at drinks parties, because almost nobody will have heard of your firm. If they have, it's because your offices are right on the High Street sandwiched between Martin the Newsagents and the Light of India takeaway, which says it all as far as they're concerned.

Other lawyers will arrogantly assume that you're at a small firm because you couldn't make the grade at a big one.

None of this necessarily matters. What do you care about prestige? Your friends like you because you're nice to children and you feed stray cats. People of the opposite sex like you because you can part your hair with your tongue. What more do you want?

'Did you see the new regulations on partnership capital accounts? Quite fascinating, I must say.'

'We got round S27 by transferring stock to Stein's dog and letting it take the short-swing profits.'

'The question is — what effect does an eclipse of the sun have on the 'market overt' doctrine.'

<u>Tax Lawyer</u>
Passionless eyes. Hates small talk. Would have become an actuary if he'd had more personality. Motto: 'The Code is Lord.'

<u>Corporate Lawyer</u>
Young partner at City mega-firm. Promises that one of these days he's going to meet his two-year-old son. Motto: 'Sleep is dispensable.'

<u>Academic Lawyer</u>
Jurisprudence is where it's at. Turned on by statute books. Has lectured in same jacket for six years. Motto: 'Anything to get published.'

'About your sister's cottage. We don't normally do residential work, of course, but in this case...'

'So I said to Jagger, 'Mick, baby, never sign anything without running it by me first'.'

'Maybe my client shot a few people, maybe he didn't. But there's a principle at issue here.'

Property Lawyer
No.1 recession-victim, struggling to fill timesheet. Lives in terror of partnership announcements. Motto: 'Don't expect me to go quietly.'

Music Lawyer
Pop star manqué. Basks in reflected glory of clients, denying the banality of what he does for them. Motto: 'I can relate.'

Litigation Lawyer
Hired gun and proud of it. Even trivial cases consume a forest of giant redwoods in document copying. Motto: 'Concede nothing.'

The Big Firm

At a big firm, the story on partnership is very different – not necessarily better, but different.

Prestige

If your firm is big enough, strangers you run into at legal conventions will have heard of it. They won't necessarily be impressed, because your firm may be so big that its letterhead appears to have all the exclusivity of a petition against government cuts. But they will have heard of it.

Another reason they might not be impressed is that they will understand what you had to sacrifice to become a partner at that firm. More importantly, they will understand the limited nature of the benefits there. Why *limited*? Because an essential fact of life in the big firms today is: *Partnership ain't what it used to be.*

Job Security

Gone are the days when partnership meant tenure for life and an impressive share of partnership profits. Less productive partners in the big firms are being forced retire early – or just plain fired. It used to be understood that the whole point of working like a slave – the expression at big firms is 'work like an associate' – was to be able, eventually, to slow down. No longer.

Life at a big firm isn't like a village egg-and-spoon race, with separate prizes for each age group, spirited slaps on the back for the fallers, and everyone getting together after-wards for a few beers. It's more like an Olympic marathon, where there's only one division – the all or nothing division – and if you can't keep up with the youngest and the fastest, you're out.

Note, however, that there's one key difference between the big-firm race and the Olympic marathon: in the big-firm race, there's no finish line. You run flat-out till you drop.*

Autonomy

Well, you say, at least there's the autonomy, the control of your own destiny – partnership at a big firm guarantees that.

You're kidding, right?

If you picture yourself as Sir Frank Crisp (co-founder of London mega-firm Ashurst, formerly known as Ashurst Morris Crisp) when you fantasise about becoming a partner, then

---

* According to a survey undertaken by the *Mail on Sunday* on Karoshi (death by overwork) back in 1991, 7.7 per cent of all solicitors who died in that year were aged between thirty-five and forty-four. The national average for this age group was 1.7 per cent. Things haven't improved since.

the chances are you also picture yourself as Caesar when you fantasise about Ancient Rome. But making you partner doesn't make you Caesar, it barely gets you a place on the terraces at the Coliseum.

It's the very nature of a partnership that everything is subject to vote. Therefore, you *are* vulnerable to being removed, and the partnership can, if it has the collective will, control everything from how much holiday you take to what colour carpet you have in your office. If they decide to move against you, your individual vote will be about as useful and valuable as, well, as your vote in a General Election.

You can't take on a new client, or even a new matter for an old client, without checking with everyone else that there are no conflicts with existing work. For that matter, the other partners can veto your new client if they don't like his looks or his politics – or his lawyer.

To add insult to injury, everything you do in a big firm is monitored and evaluated, and reduced to performance statistics. Even when you're one of the bosses! Is it part of your game plan to reach sixty and still have to simulate hard work when what you really feel like is a quiet kip at your desk?

THE RAINMAKER

Every lawyer wants to be a rainmaker. Rainmakers run the ship. If the other partners don't toe the line the way the rainmaker wants them to, the rainmakers can walk, and pull the partnership to bits. It happens all the time.

A few rainmakers pull in clients by their proven track record as lawyers. Most of them get clients through personal connections, and have the work done for them by senior associates or non-rainmaking partners. The fact is, if you can bring in heavyweight clients, you don't need to know a lot of law. You don't need to know how to read.

But don't you at least have to supervise the associates and non-rainmaking partners who are doing your work? Don't you have to review and edit the mountains of documents and advice letters they turn out? There's no need. They're better at it than you are. All you have to do is sign the documents and show up at the occasional meeting — enough to keep your clients from realising just how low down the evolutionary ladder you are.

Money

At one time a partner's pay was based largely – or even solely – on seniority. Other things being equal, more seniority meant more pay.

Today you might find yourself getting *less* money with each passing year, rather than more. It just depends on how the partnership wants to divide the cake.

Couldn't you increase your share somewhat by working a little harder in a given year? Aside from the fact that you're probably already working harder than the human cardiovascular system can bear, it's up to the partnership which might (or might not) choose to reward your additional labour.

Make no mistake: the money that comes with partnership at a big firm is likely to be substantial.* But put it into perspective: there are 26-year-old dealers in the City making over £1,000,000 a year and innumerable investment bankers making four or five times that sum.

And, perhaps more relevant, the money that a just-made-up partner receives isn't a great deal more than what a senior associate makes, which suggests that there's nothing intrinsically magical on the other side of the partnership line.

---

* The most profitable UK law firm in 2011, according to *City AM* magazine, was Slaughter & May with gross fees of £439.5 million. Its 126 partners were paid an average of £1.84 million for their efforts, making them among the highest paid lawyers anywhere in the world.

CHAPTER 9

ELEMENTS OF STYLE: THE LAWYERLY LOOK

A wardrobe as dull as your work

There are various points of style every lawyer should observe. For associates these points can gain you critical mileage in the minds of the vast majority of partners who will never see your work and who know you only socially – or antisocially, as the case may be. For partners, the idea is essentially the same – there is always someone more senior you need to impress.

Arguably, it doesn't matter much how lawyers look: after all, they spend most of their time in their offices, and when they do get out it's usually just to see their counterparts at other firms. Still, unless you've already given up hope of a better life, it's worth paying some attention to how you appear.

The Men

Conservatism should be your watchword. This doesn't mean

you have to be stuffy. Your suits can run the whole gamut from blue to black, with occasional narrow pinstripes for a festive touch. Single-breasted suits are preferred.

Shirts should be plain coloured or in narrow single-colour stripes. You might personally favour alternating cerise and canary-yellow stripes half an inch wide, or have a penchant for Indonesian batik, but partners will view such gaudy flamboyance with deep suspicion.

If the hair on your chest is thicker than three week old yoghurt, make sure your shirt is 'Oxford' cotton rather than ultra-fine Egyptian cotton. Your rug may work wonders in Cowes Week, but it looks terrible poking out between your shirt buttons. Particularly on women.

Shirt collars should generally not be button-down. Again, partners distrust anything that smacks of foreign, particularly American, dress codes. They think a Brooks Brothers shirt is just the start of an inevitable slide down the formality scale, and that if they don't nip it in the bud, their associates will turn up for work wearing those funny loafers with tassels on them, and using Donald Trump-style negotiation techniques.

Ties should be narrower than the prevailing standard, whatever it is. Silk, not nylon, and if they have to have a motif, preferably something a little more sophisticated than that of your University Honking club. Stripes and spots are fine, but don't get cute with one of those trompe l'oeil numbers – apart from the fact that they look like dead fish hanging down your shirt, they are often 'hand painted' which throws into doubt their ability to hold beer, coffee and saliva stains without smudging.

Accessories, like clothes, should be confined to the plain and practical. If you've always dreamed of wearing a Mont Blanc Meisterstuck in your breast pocket, carrying your documents around in a Louis Vuitton wallet and whipping out your iPad to do some spreadsheet analysis consider whether you're in the wrong game. Real lawyers are brand-ignorant and strictly utilitarian in their choice of products, and any unnecessary ornament tends to be frowned upon.

Wear a simple watch: you really don't need one that tells you the time in Tokyo, nor one that tracks your nitrogen decompression rate below seventy metres.

It is worth keeping *one* decent pen on you, however, for that rare occasion when a partner turns to you for something with which to sign a contract – you don't want to have to fish through your trouser pockets only to come up with a tooth-marred biro with lint balls caught in the clip.

The Women

Except at the stuffiest London firms (which is to say, the stuffiest firms in the world), it is now okay for women to wear dresses rather than suits. This represents progress. Until not so long ago, women in the law felt compelled to look like men. Now they just feel compelled to *act* like men.

Otherwise, the rules of drabness are the same. Your attire should match the job. Make-up should be minimised and perfume avoided altogether. You don't want to encourage the senior partner to think of you in the same vein as the women in Paris he knew in his youth.

Hemlines should stay at or below the knees (or partners' eyes won't). Shun dresses with slits up the sides unless (a) you have great legs, and (b) you're looking for promotion to receptionist.

Your hairstyle should be inconspicuous, preferably gathered up in a wad at the back. Anything too stylish will give the impression you spend a lot of time fussing with it when you should be working.

Shoe heels should be low, if not flat. High heels will just cause you to be confused with secretaries.

Large breasts should be avoided. Partners will stare.

The Briefcase

Carry a large expandable black one. No *business* person would be caught dead carrying such a monster – someone else handles their grunt work – but lawyers *thrive* on grunt work. They take pride in walking out of their offices on Friday night with two of these briefcases, each one big enough to hold a human body.

You should do the same. It's all part of cultivating the proper image. You needn't actually have anything in your case, although some file documents are handy just in case you find yourself sitting next to a partner on the train in the morning. Pulling out a copy of *Viz* just won't do.

REAL LAWYERS EAT FAST FOOD

A law degree and success in the LPC do not a *real* lawyer make. There's more to being a real lawyer — such as messing up sentences by reversing the subject and predicate (see preceding sentence).

How can you tell if you're a Real Lawyer, a Sylvester Stallone or an Arnold Schwarzenegger of a lawyer? Measure yourself by the following criteria:

Real lawyers eat fast food.
The faster, the better — and preferably something you can eat at your desk. Eating just gets in the way of work.

Real lawyers don't have tans.
They prefer the library to the beach. It's not easy drafting a prospectus while lying in the sand.

Real lawyers don't drive flashy cars.
Rainmakers might, but nobody said they're real lawyers. Real lawyers aren't into style or ostentation.

Real lawyers don't have beards.
Not even the men. Beards are bushy and untidy. Even a moustache looks too much like nose hairs out of control.

Real lawyers don't have erotic daydreams.
They don't have trouble concentrating on their work. For a real lawyer, tax reports are erotic enough to hold their attention.

Real lawyers love to proofread — everything.
Not just legal documents and formal correspondence. Real lawyers proofread street signs, food labels, menus, even the lists of personalised number plates that appear in Saturday's *Daily Mail*. Nothing makes their day like catching a typo.

Real lawyers don't like children.
Children are noisy, frivolous, distracting. They just don't care about the important things in life – Mem & Arts, Directors' Liability, the *White Book* etc...

Real lawyers like fact, not fiction.
Too often novels depend for their storyline on coincidental events, and lawyers just can't accept that. They can't see the point. They like hard information, untainted by the intrusion of an author's imagination.

CHAPTER 10

THE BAR

Grown men in wigs, gowns
and stockings – what's not to like?

One of the many questions you will have to ask yourself at the start of your legal career is – do I want to be a barrister or a solicitor? For most students, the answer is simple. There are many more opportunities to find work as a solicitor as the profession is so much larger and it is therefore by far the safer, more sensible option. However, for those who like the idea of courtroom advocacy, public schoolboys (and girls), chambers that feel a good deal like Oxbridge colleges, wigs, gowns and – for elderly gentlemen – silk stockings, then the Bar is the place for you.

Choosing an Inn
Your first decision is – which Inn of Court shall I join? There are four Inns – Gray's Inn, Lincoln's Inn, Middle Temple and Inner Temple, and they are very similar. An old piece of doggerel goes as follows:

Middle for the Rich Man

Inner for the Poor
Lincoln's for the Foreigner
Gray's for the Bore.

In truth it really doesn't matter – any Inn will do and all grant the impoverished student access to well-funded scholarships and bursaries which can help offset the ruinous cost of a legal education. You also have to eat a certain number of dinners in hall – most students do this grudgingly but the smart ones will note that a three-course meal served with claret and port (and even snuff afterwards if who know whom to ask) at highly subsidised rates can be an excellent way to mitigate the otherwise grey landscape of a legal education. Best of all you get to take your meals in a superb imitation of the Hogwarts dining hall.

Pupillage

Prospective barristers must apply for pupillage in barristers' chambers – essentially a kind of apprenticeship system in which senior barristers instruct the young and eager in the mysteries of the Bar – such as why gentlemen's suits should have four buttons on the cuffs (apparently they should – but no one can explain why) and why barristers never, ever shake hands with one another. Pupils are assigned to 'pupil masters', who take on the burden of training the young out of a sense of duty and obligation – and certainly not because they like it. Do not fool yourself into thinking that your newly learned legal skills will be of any use to them at all. They won't be. Your principal tasks will be to fetch their dry cleaning and make tea. Otherwise, keep quiet and try not to say anything that might convince them of your utter unsuitability for a career as a barrister.

It is at the pupillage stage where things get tough. The Bar is massively oversubscribed and places are hard to come by. Worse still, not just any chambers will do. Many sets of chambers struggle to survive on declining legal aid rates funded by an ever-leaner public purse, and their members are lucky to get paid as much as a plumber. Actually, many make far less than the average plumber.

Of course, some chambers do very well indeed – especially a handful of famed 'commercial' sets, which include QCs (Queen's Counsel – an honorific term for an especially experienced and expensive barrister) who can make millions of pounds in fees each year, serving large corporations and wealthy clients in a lot of trouble. Getting a pupillage in such chambers is difficult and winning the holy grail of a tenancy – essentially a job for life –

can seem virtually impossible. The road is long and hard, and only those with Oxbridge Firsts need apply.

Getting a Pupillage

Once upon a time being the nephew of the Lord Chief Justice could get you in on a nod and a wink – but nowadays the Bar is as politically correct as the *Guardian Educational Supplement*. What you really need these days is points on your CV: debating contests (known obscurely as '*moots*'), essay writing competitions (such as those organised by *The Times*), part-time work at the Law Centre or the Free Representation Unit – all of these are vital ways of proving your commitment and setting you apart from the clamouring herd. Academic prowess alone will not win you the keys to the kingdom. In the end the real trick is to know your own level. Aim too high and you will find yourself out-competed by leaner smarter candidates. Aim too low and you'll get a tenancy – but you'll be doing legal aid work in the Slough Family Court for the rest of your days.

The Clerks

One of the odder features of life at the Bar is the barrister's relationship with his clerk. Although The old days when the Head Clerk took 10 per cent of the earnings of everyone in Chambers – and could thereby acquire riches beyond the dreams of most barristers – are long gone, senior clerks remain well-rewarded, well respected, and a serious force to be reckoned with in every set of chambers. Even in those advanced sets with twenty-first century 'practice managers', the clerks still run the show.

No matter how junior the barrister nor how senior the clerk, the barrister (even a most lowly pupil) is addressed as *Mr* Bloggs, while the barrister addresses the clerk by his first name. Respect and formality on the one side, familiarity on the other. This can be especially uncomfortable for pupils, generally not used to hearing their family name in social discourse since their headmaster told them off at school, and suddenly faced with apparent deference from someone many years their senior. Do not be fooled by this outward sign of respect. The clerks have as much respect for pupils as do most barristers in chambers (i.e. none) and they wield considerable power over junior barristers' careers. Chambers may offer a pupil a job, but it's the clerks who decide who gets the work.

Getting a Tenancy

Winning a tenancy is the hardest part of all. You went into the Bar because you have a naturally combative nature, a free spirit

– a desire to challenge authority and make your voice heard. Forget all that. As a pupil barrister your goal is to be meek, mild and utterly inoffensive. Far more important than who supports you in chambers is who is against you – just one strong voice against your candidacy and you're hunting for your 'third six' – barrister speak for the slow train to oblivion.

The odds against you are much higher than they would be at a firm of solicitors, where most of those on 'training contracts' will expect to get kept on, unless times are ruinously tough. At the Bar, most chambers will take just one or two promising candidates, even though there may be numerous pupils competing for a spot. Each pupil is pitted against his or her contemporaries in a Darwinian struggle for survival, and the experience of being a pupil barrister is enjoyed by no one – not even the successful candidates.

Being a Barrister

Once you have stormed the barricades and been invited into the inner sanctum, most barristers are dismayed to discover that work is often hard to come by. Barristers' clerks can make or break your career and there is no guarantee of receiving 'instructions' from solicitors. Worse, solicitors rarely pay on time. Fees can dribble in months and even years after the work was originally undertaken. Some fees simply never get paid at all.

Gradually all barristers realise that what now actually awaits them is a lifetime of ingratiating themselves with the firms of solicitors who can send them work and keep them from descending into genteel poverty, ever envious of their friends who went into investment banking instead. Horror of horrors – the Bar turns out to be a business just like any other.

Advocacy

What barristers do, and for the most part do well, is courtroom advocacy, that is to say the job of conducting and fighting a trial or hearing. Two decades ago the government removed the restrictions on solicitors appearing in the higher courts – in the face of strenuous opposition from that most eloquent of trade unions, the Bar Council, who predicted an end to justice as we know it. The government got its way, and justice survived (somehow or other), but a funny thing happened. Or rather, didn't happen. Solicitors did not, on the whole take over the barrister's role as specialists in courtroom advocacy. The Bar lost its monopoly, but not its job. Why? Because courtroom advocacy is what barristers do, and for the most part they are very good at it.

Appearing in court for the first time varies from being completely terrifying to just plain awful. Baby barristers are well advised to get as much practice at this as early as possible. Debates, moots, mock trials, pro bono work for the Free Representation Unit – anything that will cure your fears at the earliest opportunity should be attempted. You *will* be terrified and you *will* be useless, but be terrified and useless when you're not accompanied by a paying client who is sitting right behind you.

An old saw goes that there are three secrets of advocacy: 'preparation, preparation and preparation'. This is fine in theory, but in practice barristers regularly receive their briefs the night before a trial in which they have never met the client and know nothing about the case. If you get one of these on your first day, find the nearest experienced and kindly face and beg them for help. On the morning of the trial, find the court clerk and ask them to let the judge know it's your first day. Judges remember what it was like – and they will sympathise. No one ever forgets their first day.

CHAPTER 11

ALTERNATIVE LEGAL CAREERS

(1) civil service (2) country practice

Private practice in an urban law factory isn't the only route. Some of the finest lawyers around opt for legal work in the civil service – or head for the hills.

The Civil Service Lawyer

The primary advantage of being a lawyer in the civil service is early, hands-on responsibility – none of these two-year warm-up periods before getting to argue some piddling motion for extension of time in a county court.

A civil service salary is nothing to shout about, particularly in comparison with what some lawyers make in private practice. And you shouldn't be too particular about your creature comforts. Civil service lawyers required to travel are sometimes surprised to discover that there's a class lower than 2nd on Network South East – and it's no fun at all if you're allergic to animals.

But if you measure income in pounds *per hour*, it's far from clear who comes out on top. If private firms spawned the concept of the 25-hour working day, government lawyers spawned the concept of the 25-hour working week.

Being a civil service lawyer just might be right for you – no private firm has a bigger client – but don't make any rash decisions. Read the following rules on survival as a civil service lawyer, and be sure you know what you're letting yourself in for:

Insist on Having Your Own Desk

Nothing is certain in the civil service. It is too much to hope for a private office, but demand your own desk. In fact, negotiate this before you accept the job.

Brush up Your Secretarial Skills

If you got through law school without learning how to type, now is the time to learn. The good news is typing skills are not beyond the competence of even a techno-peasant like yourself – after all, you've been addicted to Facebook for the last five years. The bad news is that there's a reason such skills are, well, simple. Read on:

There are a number of perfectly competent secretaries working in the civil service (people debate whether the number is two or three), but you will not get one right away – say, within your first ten years. You will get another kind, to whom filing her (or his) fingernails is more important than filing your papers.

Do not be too harsh in judging these secretaries. They work under trying conditions – handling five lawyers' work output between the hours of ten and three-thirty with an hour and a half for lunch takes some doing. In judging them, consider how your own performance would suffer if you wore iPod earphones all day.

Secretarial self-reliance is essential to survival in government practice. You don't have to be able to take apart and reassemble a photocopier, but it wouldn't hurt. You will invariably be the next person to use the machine after someone has dropped a box of paperclips in its guts. Note: when the lights start blinking, do not panic – leave the room quietly and find another machine.

Dress Functionally

Dress is not as important in the civil service as it is in private practice: a government salary can't support a Bond Street wardrobe, and let's face it, who wants to wear a £750 suit behind a £95 IKEA desk.

Avoid Drift

The pace of the civil service can be pleasantly slow, to say the least. You will undoubtedly be tempted, on a prolonged basis, to relax, settle back, borrow your secretary's iPod, and give no thought to the future.

Resist this temptation. You're there to learn and advance, not drift. The civil service has a thousand dead ends – somebody has to write those regulations governing the composition of sausage meat – and you don't want to find yourself stranded.

Don't assume it will be obvious when your career has come to a halt. Unlike the private sector, the civil service doesn't operate on an up-or-out system. You might be doing the same thing in thirty years that you were when you began. (If you have any doubts about the effect of this on your mental agility, try having a conversation with the 'lifer' at the end of the hall.)

At a minimum, learn skills that are transferable to the private sector, such as litigation skills. Reviewing documents under the Official Secrets Act might be exciting for two days, maybe three, but a year of it could turn you into a civil service lawyer forever.

Country Practice

The joy of being a lawyer out in the boondocks is that you're as much a feature of country life as the postman on his bicycle, the retired couple who run the pub, the old folk sitting on the village bench, and the yobs from the local estate who make everyone else's life a misery. You're part of the fabric of the community.

The *problem* with being a country lawyer is that you're also part psychologist, part family therapist, and maybe part plumber and animal midwife. You're expected to *join in* with community activities, which means compulsory morris dancing on Saturday mornings at best, and being cast as the back legs of the panto donkey for three years running at worst.

Depending on your tastes, the balance may be a positive one. Whatever country pursuits you're press-ganged into, who's to say it's worse than being told to perform anatomically impossible acts on yourself on the London Underground each morning. (If the mugger is armed, you may find the acts aren't impossible.)

The major difference between the practice of a City lawyer and a country lawyer or even a suburban lawyer, is the level of perfection that goes into each job. City lawyers attempt a perfect job on every project, no matter how disproportionate the costs are to the stakes involved. They'll not only produce an eighty page lease for a tiny unit on an industrial estate, but also spend thousands pounds of their client's money proofreading the lease.

Country and suburban lawyers don't do this because their clients are individuals or small businesses who just can't afford it. They have to do something that City lawyers *never* have to do: pull in the reins, perform a cost-benefit analysis, exercise some *judgement*.

CHAPTER 12

LEGAL WRITING

Excuse me, but what does this say in English?

Everyone knows that legal writing is different from normal writing. People can understand normal writing.

Legal writing is instantly recognisable. There's no mistaking a 'whereas' or a 'forthwith'.

You can spot a 'hereinafter referred to as' miles away. (Talk about floccinaucinihilipilification!)

Why do lawyers write like this? Several reasons.

First, they like big words. Lots of people like big words, but dealing with them ten to twelve hours a day affects your brain, altering your perspective on what is sesquipedalian and what isn't.

A lawyer will say 'vehicle' when he means 'car', and he will say 'practicable' when he means 'practical'. (No one outside the law has even heard of the word 'practicable'.)

The second trait that makes lawyers write so peculiarly is that they are exceedingly meticulous by nature. This translates not only into aberrant eating habits but also into an unnatural fear of ambiguity and a craving for precision in their prose.

Take the following sentence, which might appear in papers relating to a charge of living off immoral earnings:

> Instead of running an hotel on the premises, the Defendant company decided to set up a brothel, which is the subject of the present proceedings.

This sentence would distress most lawyers because of the pronoun 'which' in the fourth line. The average lawyer would be worried about its ambiguity: does 'which' refer to the brothel? To the Defendant company? To the morality of their operation?

The mere hint of a possibility of confusion would torture the lawyer's conscience. The same obsession with order that led him to colour-code his notes in law school would lead him to rewrite the sentence as follows:

> Instead of running an hotel on the premises, the Defendant company decided to set up a brothel, *which brothel* is the subject of the present proceedings.

The additional word adds nothing but length to the sentence. It distracts the reader by its unnatural placement.

But a lawyer would always say *which brothel* just as he would always say *which contract, which court,* or *which* anything else he could think of. The extra word satisfies his infancy-based urge to keep things neat and tidy. With it, he'll sleep soundly tonight, gurgling and cooing, at peace with the world.

The third trait that accounts for lawyers' bizarre writing style is their innate conservatism. The average lawyer is not bold by nature. His ambition is to go through life with his arse fully covered. To this end he qualifies everything he writes, instinctively fearful of being caught in an exaggeration or even a metaphor.

'SPEAKING AS A LAWYER...'

Lawyers often preface their remarks with 'Speaking as a lawyer...' Is this a boast? A disclaimer?

Whatever it is, it's unnecessary. It's obvious when someone is 'speaking as a lawyer'.

For one thing, lawyers over-enunciate their words, smacking their lips and pronouncing each syllable crisply and distinctly, as if talking to someone for whom English isn't a mother tongue.

This can be irritating. Sometimes it makes you want to insert their tongues into the office shredder.

Lawyers also talk in uncommonly full, formal sentences. They take pains to select just the right words for their thoughts, with mid-sentence pauses so long you could squeeze in a quick reading of *War and Peace* in the interval. It's as if they're talking on the record — for posterity.

A lot posterity cares.

'The sky is blue'

Stylistic peculiarities are particularly evident in the way partners edit anything produced by trainees or associates.

Every partner thinks he's a bit of a wordsmith. There is no sentence so straightforward that he will not happily torture beyond any recognition. Take the sentence 'The sky is blue.'

Please.

No first year trainee would be so naive as to think that this proposition could pass muster in a big firm. If she made it through law school, she knows enough to say 'The sky is *generally* blue.'

Better still, 'The sky generally *appears* blue.'

For extra syllables, 'The sky generally appears *to be* blue.'

A senior associate seeing this sentence might take pity on the trainee and explain that before showing it to his partner, she should put it in a more 'lawyerly' form. At the very least, the sentence should be revised to say '*In some parts of the world*, the sky generally appears to be blue.'

Armed with these qualifiers, the trainee thinks herself protected. Her conversation with her partner will proceed thus:

PARTNER HURST: 'You say here that in some parts of the world what is thought of as the sky generally appears to be blue. I assume this is an early draft. Could I see the final version?

TRAINEE CARTER: Uh, that's all I've done so far... What exactly do you mean?

PARTNER HURST: Well, it's a bit bald, isn't it? I mean, just to come out and assert it as fact.

TRAINEE CARTER: I'm sorry? Are we talking about the same thing?

PARTNER HURST: Well, this business about the sky – what do you mean by the sky?

TRAINEE CARTER: Well, I mean what I see when I look up ... at least when I'm outside. Isn't that what everybody sees?

PARTNER HURST: Well, if you *mean* only when you're outside, you should say so. Herbert Smith would love to rip us apart on that kind of mistake. And what about at night? Even at night? I see stars at night – are they blue? Do you mean everything *but* stars, or do you mean when there are no stars out?

TRAINEE CARTER: I suppose I mean during the day.

PARTNER HURST: You *suppose*. Susan, this is serious business. We can't go around supposing things. Besides, what about the sun? If it's daytime, the sun will be out, or do you know something I don't?

TRAINEE CARTER: Well, of course I ... I mean, no, I don't ... but no one in his right mind stares at the sun. They'd go blind.

PARTNER HURST: What support do you have for this comment about 'some parts of the world'? *Which* parts? Does it have to be stated so broadly? Can't we just say 'In London' or wherever we mean?

TRAINEE CARTER: That sounds fine to me. I just never thought anyone would challenge... I mean, who would disagree with...

PARTNER HURST: And what do you mean by 'generally thought of?' Thought of by whom exactly? Lawyers? Scientists? Pigeons? For goodness sake, Stephanie, this has more holes in it than Swiss cheese. I haven't seen such sloppiness in all my years at Cower, Cringe & Tremble. Take it away and come up with something a little better thought out.

10 PRINCIPLES OF LEGAL WRITING

1. Never use one word where ten will do.
2. Never use a small word where a big one will suffice.
3. Never use a simple statement where it appears that one of substantially greater complexity will achieve similar goals.
4. Never use plain English where Latin, *mutatis mutandis*, will do.
5. Qualify virtually everything.
6. Do not be embarrassed about repeating yourself.
7. Do not be embarrassed about repeating yourself.
8. Worry about the difference between 'that' and 'which'.
9. Never refer to one's opponent's 'arguments' — he makes 'assertions', and they are always 'bold'.
10. If a lay person can read a document from beginning to end without falling asleep, it needs work.

Even more startling for new trainees than this distortion of English by verbally incontinent old-timers is the process by which a legal 'case' is assembled.

Law students are taught that judges decide cases on the basis of (a) statute, and (b) existing authority. As far as case authority is concerned, the system is supposedly ruled by precedent. Accordingly, students assume that the way lawyers construct their argument is by researching previous cases and applying the present facts to them.

What really happens is that partners, in collusion with the barrister they have instructed, write the arguments *first*. They know what they want to say; they know how their argument has to turn out.

The file is then passed to a trainee or associate or the barrister's pupil, with each assertion followed by a bracketed note '[Find case support for this statement]'.

This process obviously assumes that there *is* case support out there for any statement. There is.

If you ever get charged with this stunningly demoralising task, make sure you don't overlook one of these references. For some reason, judges get upset when they find remarks in the case documentation like 'Cite the usual crap'.

What about those few propositions so obscure or implausible that no authority can be found for them –even by the army of associates which big firms readily commit to the task? You can't just abandon them. You take a deep breath, put them up front and call them 'self-evident'.

CHAPTER 13

DRAFTING LEGAL DOCUMENTS

More is better – unless it begins to make sense

Lawyers like to think there's something special about the way they 'draft' legal documents. The word itself suggests refined skills, even artistic capabilities. They know that any old fool can, in time, learn to write letters weighed down with legal mumbo-jumbo, but to draft a really good lease agreement you've got to have the sort of back-to-front upside-down mind of a theoretical physicist.

Drafting truly impenetrable documents is not easy. Many young lawyers' initial attempts are rejected outright by partners who offer helpful comments like: 'This won't do Williams. I can still get the gist of some of the sentences.'

Fortunately, most kinds of documents have been drafted hundreds, even thousands of times before. The large law firms keep digital copies of the most common precedents on their servers, and have heaving shelves full of every other conceivable kind. An associate who is asked to produce a lease for a client's new office block just has to go through the precedents. Then he fills in the blanks.

Let's face it – a trainee in his first week could do it. Trainees in their first week *do* do it.

Sole practitioners and small law firms don't usually have such extensive or well-organised precedent banks, but that doesn't mean they have it any harder. There are numerous books for sale with model contracts, leases and wills of every imaginable sort, and innumerable websites selling the same.

If your client is a Hindu who wants to leave all his possessions to his sacred cow, the precedent books will have several versions of the form you need. Just fill in the name and address of the cow.

TYPES OF LEGAL DOCUMENTS

There are only four types of legal documents:
1. boring;
2. extremely boring;
3. comatose; and
4. pull-the-plug-and-let-me-die-with-dignity.

There are four types of lawyers who produce these documents:
1. boring
2. extremely boring;
3. comatose; and
4. those for whom the plug has been pulled.

The last are easy to spot. They're the ones with all the dignity.

Notwithstanding this simplicity, legal documents come in a dazzling array. Whether you need something to finalise the terms of a deal or, more importantly, to put under the short leg of your desk, you have an impressive smorgasbord to choose from.

In part this reflects the complexity of modern transactions, in part lawyers' zeal for their trade. It also reflects the rabbit-like creative powers of legal documents. Left alone in a drawer at night, leases beget sub-leases, wills beget trusts, deeds beget mortgages, debentures beget subordinate convertibles — with a fecundity of biblical proportions.

Thus far, the only known form of birth control is a client who refuses to pay his legal bill — which reveals in yet another context the merit of learning to 'just say no.'

How to Draft a Contract from Scratch

Drafting requires most skill on those rare occasions when a client wants to do something that's never been done before. In such circumstances, you can't just do a rehash of an old precedent. You have to obfuscate on your own.

Here's how to go about it: first, describe in normal language whatever it is your client wants to do. Then lengthen it.

A good way to begin this lengthening process is to make express provision for every conceivable turn of events, no matter how remote. Be sure to stipulate which party is at risk if an outbreak of malaria among Indonesian cane harvesters jeopardises the market for vintage Jaguars, particularly if the contract deals with office space in Birmingham.

Continue the lengthening process by defining the obvious and qualifying the irrelevant.

With regard to definitions, don't hesitate to define things in improbable ways. A good lawyer feels no compunction about defining 'person' as a 'corporation, partnership and/or livestock'; a 'car' as an 'aeroplane, balloon and/or bicycle'; and 'cash' as 'stocks, bonds and whisky.'

Don't be satisfied just with hundreds of useless definitions and qualifications. Go through it again and again, expanding clauses and inserting redundancies. This will enable you to avoid the perils of clarity inherent in forms of punctuation like the full stop.

Once you have revised your original description to the point where no one without a PhD in semantics and sophistry will know what's going on, the next step is to break it down into numerous paragraphs, sub-paragraphs and sub-sub-paragraphs, ad infinitum. This way, the various units can refer back and forth to each other ('as provided hereinabove in subsection 43(d)-4(g)(l)(A)(viii), save for sub-section Q-3(a) thereof'), thus eliminating any hint of continuity or readability.

By the time you've completed these steps, your contract should defy analysis by secret service cryptologists. All that remains is to add a few 'exhibits', 'attachments' and 'appendices'. These don't have to be relevant to anything. They're for bulk – roughage for your legal digestive tract.

The pinnacle of the art is to have an attachment to an exhibit to an appendix, with cross-references to documents not even included.

DRAFTING AND PUNCTUATION: THE PERILS OF FULL STOPS

A full stop marks the end of a sentence. This is clearly understood. That is why they should be avoided. Commas, too, tend to clarify rather than obfuscate, and they are discouraged for the same reason.

God only knows the proper use of a colon. And a semi-colon is only half of that. Their indeterminacy makes them valuable tools from your point of view, giving you the power to extend sentences almost indefinitely. With liberal and utterly random use, subjects can be separated from objects by as many sides of diarrhoeic text as you care to insert between them.

Dashes and brackets too, if properly employed, can generate a nicely convoluted sentence. Brackets within brackets, in particular, can demand endless checking-up and re-reads by the hapless reader.

But far more important than anything you say in a document is whether you are consistent in your use of letters, numbers and Roman numerals. The same lawyers who view a readable contract as beneath contempt become distraught if they come across a bungled cross-reference, forwards or backwards.

Revising documents is therefore fraught with danger. If you eliminate or, more likely, add a single clause or paragraph early on, all subsequent numbers and letters are thrown out of kilter. That is why you see so many amendments and addenda at the *end* of documents. Lawyers are terrified of making a hash of the numbers.

A Word of Warning

Opposing lawyers never sit down and draft a contract together. One side takes a first crack at it, then the other studies it and between them they thrash out a compromise.

If you're not the lawyer who did the first draft, remember that the most dangerous part is not what is *in* it, but what's *not in* it. An import/export agreement which fails to stipulate that English law should prevail could have you arguing your client's next breach of contract case in Bulgaria. An artificial insemination agreement that doesn't say what happens if your client's prize bull proves choosy about his dates could leave you testing your powers of advocacy before a tribunal of farmers in a barn (possibly a Bulgarian barn).

Two related points: (1) The initial draft produced by the opposing lawyer will usually be quite reasonable, provided nothing goes wrong; and (2) something always goes wrong.

If you're lucky things will go so badly wrong that the contract will prove irrelevant – where, for instance, one side goes belly-up, or both sides have breached the contract in a thousand different ways, or both sides realise that the litigation would go on so long that only their grandchildren would be around to hear the Court's decision. In these kinds of situations you may get off the hook even if you let your opposing lawyer's incredibly one-sided first draft through.

In most situations, however, the wording of the contract is critical, down to the last dotted i and crossed t. Your obligation is to make sure it has everything it should have – or you may leave the firm without everything *you* should have.

AMONG V. BETWEEN

A lawyer who doesn't know the difference between 'among' and 'between' would be better off in a more productive sector of the economy — say, professional boxing.

Until you have time to delve into this difficult but fascinating area on your own, you may be able to get by with the following rule of thumb: when the parties to a contract number three or more, the contract should recite that it is entered 'by and *among*' the parties. When there are fewer than three (usually two), the contract should recite that it is entered 'by and *between*' the parties.

Why it is not enough simply to say that the contract is entered 'by' the parties is an issue going to the very heart of the law.

Legal Machismo: Running with the Bulls at Pamplona

Lawyers like to say that words are their stock in trade. If so, they are burdened by an excess of inventory. Why are they so enamoured of length in their documents? Partly, no doubt, because most lawyers are men, and men have always been enamoured of length – a phenomenon traceable to the sense of inadequacy experienced by every young boy as he contemplates the superior weaponry of his father as Oedipal competitor. But that's for another book.

There's a touch of Hemingway in everyone. But lawyers can't run with the bulls or go deep-sea fishing, so they find surrogate manhood – and this includes the women – in their papers.

They deny the desk-bound tameness of their lives by thinking of their documents as weapons of battle. A lawyer refers to a contract of which he's particularly proud as 'bulletproof', meaning it can hold up under even the closest judicial scrutiny. Hostile takeovers are replete with talk of 'Poison Pills', 'White Knights' and 'Mexican Standoffs'. The objective is to 'wipe out' your opponents or 'blow them out of the water'.

This white-collar brand of machismo finds its most comical expression in the pride lawyers take in the length of their documents.

A lawyer boasts of a 300-page contract the way a sportsman boasts of a 300-pound fish. He will show it to his family and friends like a little boy showing off the hole he's dug in his back garden.

The difference is that the fish and the hole in the back garden didn't cost anyone thousands of pounds.

Also, if you thought about it for long enough, you could probably find something socially useful about the fish and the hole.

THE MYTH OF THE REASONABLE CONTRACT

Contracts are not neutral documents. Lawyers draft them for clients, and their terms invariably favour the client of the lawyer who drafted them.

A lease by a landlord's lawyer, for example, will provide for penalties if the tenant doesn't pay his rent on time, and capital punishment if it happens twice.

The same lease drafted by a tenant's lawyer will give the tenant a thirty-day grace period for late rent and provide for written apologies by the tenant if he doesn't pay by then.

So one-sided are most documents that lawyers' precedents often contain two versions of each type of document – one version drafted for one side, one version for the other. The lawyers could just as easily swap sides and use the other version sitting in their files.

In contract negotiations, the lawyers sit around identifying and complaining about the outrageous provisions in the other side's proposals, until ultimately they come up with a reasonable contract. The virtue of this process is that it enables each side's lawyer to give the appearance of driving a hard bargain – and then to charge an enormous fee.

CHAPTER 14

WOMEN IN THE LAW

Subpoena envy?

L aw used to be the exclusive preserve of men, but in recent years a quiet revolution has taken place. Women now significantly outnumber men at law school, and the same is true for students going on to do training contracts.

But what about where the big money is – at the partnership level in the big firms? Here too, we see a degree of change: no longer do the old guard talk fearfully of 'those funny chaps who wear lipstick and dance backwards'. At least not openly. And the ratio of women to men being made up as partners is improving every year. But the fact remains that men still vastly outnumber women at the head of the notepaper.[*]

For those of you discouraged by the distance that remains between the reality and the ideal, there may be some comfort

---

[*] Of the top 5 'Magic Circle' firms, with a total of 2,215 partners, just 323 or 14.5 per cent are women. At Freshfields women made up 12 per cent of partners and at Clifford Chance that number was 15 per cent. Source: *Daily Telegraph*, 22 June 2011

in knowing that male lawyers are nowhere nearly as chauvinistic as, say, scaffolders, Somali pirates or stockbrokers. You won't find your entrance to the conference room being greeted by lecherous wolf whistles or suggestive remarks. This is due not only to the enlightening (not to say emasculating) experiences of law school, but also to the brutal hours most lawyers put in. As with prisoners of war, their carnal urges take a backseat to the demands of sleep and food. In certain City firms, Gisele Bundchen could walk the corridors without raising an eyebrow.

Interestingly, a few lawyers respond in the opposite way, becoming sexually omnivorous, playing on anyone and everyone in the indiscriminate manner of sharks munching on the dangling legs of passengers from a just-capsized cruise liner.

But even these legal lechers don't match other industry standards, for the simple reason that lawyers are less likely to persist in the face of rejection. They know only too well the possibility of a sex-discrimination lawsuit. Also, as veterans of social rejection – most lawyers have been encountering it since they were toddlers – they know better than to hope to overcome it.

True, a few dinosaurs still find the time and energy to nurture their fear of female competition. 'Traditional' attitudes tend to linger – like dog poo that gets into the crevices of your trainers and won't come out no matter how many times you rub them on the grass or scrub them with the washing-up brush.

Faced with such attitudes, women can adopt one of three responses:

The Crusader
A sort of scorched-earth approach, this involves addressing every single offence or inequity, without regard to size or context. The main problem is that it requires so much energy. It's a noble battle, but exhausting.

The Mata Hari

A few women, motivated by frustration or contempt (or both), undertake to exploit those feminine resources that male partners appear most willing to recognise and reward. You can spot a hard-core Mata Hari by her black silk stockings and low-buttoned shirt.

The Survivor

This pragmatic approach consists of equal parts diplomacy, competence, thick skin and sense of humour: 'Certainty, I'll get you some coffee, Mr Hart – if you'll pick up some tampons for me when you go to lunch.'

It involves not letting your core values feel threatened in situations that require you to endure a conversation about, for instance, whether Fabio Capello should have played a 2-2-4 formation with a holding man up front during the World Cup qualifiers.

Whichever attitude you adopt, take comfort in two things: first, even the most bigoted old boys find it hard to sustain the myth of male superiority when confronted with the evident failure of the male-run criminal justice system over the past quarter century.

Second, women not only make up over half of all new entrants to the profession, but they are getting into, and excelling at, the top law firms. They represent an increasingly high proportion of the partners made up each year, and not just in the traditional 'soft' branches of the law. As they continue their inexorable advance into every area of the profession (proving slowly but surely that they can be every bit as dull and obsessive-compulsive as men) and as they ascend to control of the *client* companies, their success in the law will surely be consolidated.

In the course of researching a previous edition of this book, the publishers were anonymously sent an old internal memo from one of the major City firms. We publish it here, despite the threat of proceedings, to give you some idea of the way the profession used to be.

MEMORANDUM

To: All Partners
Date: 14.6.88
Re: Ladies in the Legal Profession

Partners will have noticed that ladies have been entering the profession in droves over the past five years. Apparently they just don't care what happens to their children, or who does the ironing — but that's emancipation for you.

Anyway, at a firm of our size, we need to show a certain sensitivity to these matters, and you might find the following tips of use:

Avoid the term 'girl lawyer'. It seems to cause offence (perhaps because, deep down, the kind of ladies who enter the profession wish they were chaps).

Don't ask a lady lawyer to get you coffee or tea. Ask her to ask your *secretary* to get it. It wastes time, but seems to make them feel better.

If you ever say 'damn' or 's***' in front of a lady lawyer, apologise immediately and let her know you don't expect her to be able to handle such rough language.

When you're involved in a firm social event, don't hide it from the ladies. Let them know, and emphasise the extent to which firm matters were discussed so they know their interests were considered and they feel involved.

Most lady lawyers are happiest doing matrimonial or trust work but if you want to use one for litigation, use a plain one, so that if you come up before a lady judge, you won't be disadvantaged (obviously, no lady judge is going to rule in favour of someone slimmer and prettier than herself).

When speaking to a lady judge, use the standard 'Your Honour' form of address, as in 'Is it Your Honour's time of the month?'

This respectful attitude should be maintained at appellate level. For example 'The Court below was clearly approaching its time of the month.' Or even — to demonstrate your sensitivity to the problem of sexist language — 'The trial judge was clearly approaching *his or her* time of the month.'

If you're involved in a jury trial and a lady lawyer expresses an interest in working on the case, take the time to explain that women simply aren't competitive enough for this sort of work, that the softness and innate passivity that makes them so charming renders them unsuited to the rough mood of the courtroom. There may be tears, but in the end they know it makes sense.

Many lady lawyers harbour romantic feelings towards partners — who amongst us has not, at one time or another, been the subject of a painful and obvious 'crush' on the part of one of our young trainees? It is tempting indeed to let matters progress, especially as any ensuing entertainment is tax-deductible. To avoid the appearance of sexual favouritism, however, you should first have her fired. This may seem drastic, asking you to go to all that trouble just to avoid the appearance of impropriety, but such are the burdens of membership in the fraternity.

CHAPTER 15

LAWYERS AND HUMOUR

*There are no funny lawyers – only funny
people who made a career mistake*

When corporate lawyers claim that their work is beneficial to society as a whole, it makes you wonder who's writing their material. These are funny guys!

Lawyers are not known for their scintillating wit, however, and are generally perceived as humourless, sober and drab. This perception is not entirely their fault. It is due in part to the nature of the matters on which they are consulted. You don't go to a lawyer for a periodic check-up, the way you do to a car mechanic or gynaecologist (who, by the way, should be two different people). You go to a lawyer for a divorce, a personal injury claim, a tax problem – things that seldom put a smile on your face.

Besides, who can be funny when he's totally exhausted and ready to fall face-down in his dinner? A lawyer at the end of the week is like a marathon runner on his twenty-sixth mile – tired and smelly.

The fact that lawyers are not the *source* of much laughter doesn't mean they can't enjoy a good joke told by someone else. Lawyers laugh long and hard at jokes told by judges, wealthy clients and HMRC Inspectors. They may not know many jokes, but they are able to *appreciate* jokes.

Given the comical nature of what they do (and all of what they bill) it is surprising that more professional comedians do not emerge from the ranks of associate lawyers. Charging £500 per hour for proofreading documents breeds an acute sense of the absurd.

The most peculiar aspect of humour in the life of associates is the extent to which they confine it to other associates or trainees. Partners who have been known to laugh – *out loud* – at jokes told by other partners show a marked reluctance to acknowledge humour out of the mouths of associates.

This behaviour could reflect a conscious effort to impress young lawyers with the seriousness of the firm's work. It could also reflect partners' revulsion at the thought of how associates spend their time – not an unreasonable response.

More likely, however, is that it reflects a psychological defence mechanism. Partners don't want to grow too familiar with people who they may well have to turn down for partnership at some point in the future. This phenomenon resembles the reluctance of jailers in Ancient Rome to become friendly with prisoners about to face the lions.

LEGAL GRAFFITI

There once was a lawyer named Rex,
Whose thing was too small to have sex.
When charged with exposure;
His plea on disclosure was
'De minimis non curat lex'.

CHAPTER 16

THE COURTS

Old litigators never die
– they just lose their appeal

itigators are proceduralists. They care less about who gets beheaded than whether the guillotine was well-oiled and running true on the day.

Suppose a litigator is told that his client, a handyman at the BBC, has just been charged with assault after rushing onto a chat show and pouring a bucket of water over one of the guests, say, Katie Price.

His reaction would be quite different from a normal person's. He wouldn't say 'My God, Steve, that's fantastic! What a hero!'

Instead, he would go over the facts with a fine-tooth comb, and look for an angle on which to base his case: 'Does Bob read that magazine she's always in? If so, there might be a case for diminished responsibility' or 'If she was talking about her autobiography, we might be able to argue provocation – check the tapes.'

Obviously, these questions have only a tenuous connection with justice and fairness. But to the litigator they're an essential part of the system.

What system? The so-called 'adversarial system', which rests on the premise that out of the clash of lies, truth will emerge.

The basic problem with the adversarial system is that neither party has an interest in reaching a fair result. They both play for *all* the marbles, not just a share, and in so doing obscure as much of the truth as possible.

The litigator's role in this system is to help his client obscure and obstruct. In *disclosure*, for example, where each side has the right to ask the other for documents relating to the case, does either lawyer turn to his client and say 'Give him the papers, John. We have nothing to hide'?

Of course not. The lawyers procrastinate for months, ultimately either holding back the one relevant document, or providing it at the last possible moment hidden in a train-load of irrelevant file-fodder.

Both sides' lawyers then go back and forth to the court filing applications for specific disclosure. This process takes aeons, and generates gigantic legal fees.

The amazing thing is that litigators are unembarrassed by this role. They like it. When they describe themselves as 'hired guns' they do so with *pride*.

To say the least, a litigator shouldn't be someone who is easily embarrassed or who reflects a lot about the end result of his life's labours. But a lot of young lawyers get sucked into litigation departments because that's just about all law school taught them to do. Sadly, a number of perfectly nice people, quite capable of being embarrassed, end up as litigators.

Litigation Posturing

Litigation is a form of low theatre. Pre-trial and in the trial itself, solicitors and barristers are constantly posturing and bluffing, putting on emotions which as lawyers they are quite incapable of feeling but which are calculated to enlist the support of the judge.

Occasionally lawyers on opposing sides of a case do in fact hate each other, because they have convinced themselves that they genuinely feel the passions they pretend or because they're inherently odious. More often, however, their passions are totally contrived, and they'll be buying each other drinks in the bar the moment court adjourns, only to take up cudgels the next day. Below are seven of the most common litigation poses:

Righteous Indignation
Lawyers adopt this pose to suggest that their opponent's case is not only wrong in law but also ethically questionable. They use it when there is no law on their side.

Moral Outrage
This is like righteous indignation, only stronger. It is the pose of the divorce lawyer defending a self-made tycoon who has just abandoned his 50-year-old wife for his 23-year-old secretary, and doesn't see why he should have to give up any of his hard-earned millions to support his first wife.

Disdain
This pose is adopted by lawyers defending one wealthy company against another. The idea is to convince the court that the claimant is just trying it on against your client, who obviously didn't *mean* to pour toxic waste into the kindergarten water supply.

Intimacy
This is the pose of hotshot London barristers trying to squash obscure claimants represented by even more obscure juniors

from the provinces. They use this pose, augmented by winks and hints of levity, to establish a personal relationship with the judge, suggesting without stating that *good* lawyers ('like you and me, Your Honour') can see that the claimant is a few sandwiches short of a picnic.

Bewilderment

This is the pose of the lawyer whose opponents have just scored a direct hit, and who have hammered home an argument to which he has no reply. He adopts a pose of utter bewilderment as a last-ditch effort to suggest that the argument makes little sense and is irrelevant to the facts of the case.

Sincerity

This 'would-I-lie-to-you?' pose is used by defence lawyers attempting to counter popular assumptions about the culpability of certain categories of defendant. Battling against a jury which has already made up its mind, they adopt a pose that says 'I *know* what it looks like, but believe me, Sir Henry was actually trying to get the girl *out* of his car.' Occasionally, the jury is stupid enough to fall for the act.

Disappointment

With this pose a lawyer attempts to suggest that the devastating points just scored by his opponent are, to his sadness, underhanded and deceitful. Often the lawyer will season this pose with a pinch of parental solicitude, as if for a child gone astray.

YOU AND 'THE COURT'

10 Commandments of Courtroom Conduct

1. The judge is always 'Your Honour' (County Court), 'Your Lordship' (Crown Court and High Court) or just 'The Court'.
2. The judge's clerk is always 'Your Honour' or 'The Court'.
3. The judge is never 'late', but sometimes 'the press of business' interrupts her schedule.
4. The judge's prior ruling is never 'mistaken', but a contrary ruling may well be justified by 'subsequent developments in the law'.
5. The judge is always to be thanked for her thoughtful ruling, even if she has just insulted you personally and made an exemplary damages award of £1 million against your client.
6. The judge has never 'forgotten' anything, but frequently you must 'refresh the court's recollection' of key facts.
7. The judge has never 'neglected to read the court papers' but frequently you must 'draw the court's attention' to key facts therein.
8. The judge knows every relevant statute and case, so it is of course appropriate to introduce points of law with 'As the court knows...'
9. The judge will never 'hold on' or 'wait a second', but sometimes you may 'beg the court's pardon' or 'pray for the court's momentary indulgence'.
10. The judge never has to 'visit the Ladies', but often 'the court will take a brief recess'.

A final reminder – before you go into court, remind yourself of the correct forms of address. There is nothing more humiliating than a junior barrister or solicitor addressing a High Court Judge as 'Your Worship' or a Magistrate as 'Your Lordship'.

CHAPTER 17

LEGAL ETHICS

(And other great oxymorons)

The very concept of legal ethics tends to trigger spontaneous laughter within the general populace. It is viewed as a monumental contradiction in terms, an oxymoron ranking up there with 'BT customer service', 'airline food' and 'military intelligence'.

Lawyers profess to take legal ethics very seriously. It is a required part of the professional training, and receives lip service from judges, law professors and professional organisations. For this reason if no other, and notwithstanding its irrelevance to current legal practice, every lawyer should have at least a passing familiarity with the Code of Conduct as set out by the Solicitors Regulation Authority.

The Code contains rules governing virtually every aspect of practice set down in typical lawyerly form – that is to say, lengthy, complex and unintelligible to laymen. It ranks up there with Kant's *Groundwork of the Metaphysics of Morals* as a cure for insomnia.

HOW FAR CAN YOU GO?

How far *can* you go in fulfilling your ethical obligation to represent your client diligently? Suppose your client is charged with stabbing someone in a dark alley. Can you ethically contend — indeed are you ethically *required* to contend — that he didn't actually stab the victim, but just happened to be holding the filleting knife when the victim walked into it ... backwards ... twenty-three times?

Over the years, four tests have been developed for measuring which arguments are acceptable and which go too far:

The Smell Test

The most stringent of the four standards, this one precludes you from making any argument that just doesn't smell right. Lots of arguments smell so bad that people in the courtroom will be checking the soles of their shoes.

The Blush Test

If you can make a given argument without turning visibly red, it passes. The stringency of this test, like that of the two below, varies according to the shamelessness of the lawyer. In some firms it is entirely redundant.

The Gag Test

If you can utter a theory or alibi without physically choking from the outrageousness of your words, it passes. Known colloquially as the 'Amnesia at the Check-Out' Test.

The Wrath of God Test

This is an extremely liberal test, precluding only those arguments so insupportable that their very utterance is likely to cause lightning to strike you down even as you speak. This test is usually reserved for *extremely rich* clients with a lot to lose.

Part of the Code is taken up with the sort of safety-net rules that have to be in any professional regulations 'just in case', such as:

> A solicitor shall not do anything which might compromise or impair the good reputation of the solicitor's profession.

Of course. Grass is green, the sky is blue, and vomit is disgusting.

Other rules simply wouldn't need stating if such as rule had any real restraining effect:

> A solicitor shall not take unfair advantage of a client by overcharging for work done' and shall not act 'solely to gratify a client's malice or vindictiveness.

But lawyers, as if anyone who's dealt with them didn't know, are prone to exactly the same temptations as professionals theoretically a lot lower down the ladder of trustworthiness and need constant reminding of even the most basic ethical tenets:

> To give an estimate that has been pitched at an unrealistically low level solely to attract the work, and subsequently to charge a higher fee is improper.

Of course, with architects you at least know when you're being ripped off: even complete bozos figure things aren't right when they can count the stars through the gaps in their roof extension.

Anyone who would promulgate such rules clearly has incredible faith in the power of words – the sort of person who would put a 'Do not Steal' sign under the wipers of his Bentley when he parks it in Heathrow Long-Stay for a month.

COURTESY AMONG LAWYERS

'After you, dog breath'

There was a time when lawyers were extremely polite to one another. Courtroom conduct was a model of civility and the refined intercourse of adversaries in litigation reflected Western Civilisation at its peak.

Except for the courtesies still accorded to the Bench (the so-called 'bootlick' imperative) those gentle and genteel days appear to be behind us now, as tempers go unchecked and mouths unmuzzled. A casual eavesdropper of the courtroom in the twenty-first century is likely to hear references to 'dubious assertions' and 'theories of uncertain origin'. A cursory perusal of courtroom transcripts will almost certainly turn up charges of 'unfounded allegations' and 'erroneous assumptions'.

With this kind of language already commonplace, can slurs such as 'questionable good faith' and 'tendentious mischaracterisation' be far behind?

CHAPTER 18

THE CREATIVE ART OF BILLING

Who says there are only
twenty-four hours in a day?

Anyone who says lawyers aren't imaginative hasn't seen a lawyer fill out his time-sheets.

If you hope to succeed in the law, it is essential to master the creative aspects of billing. As a trainee you can never tell your friends how you really spend your time; as an associate, you can never tell partners how you really spend your time, and as a partner you can never tell clients what they're really being billed for.

Even if you're a lay person, it is important to understand the billing process. You'll still end up in hock to your lawyer, but at least you'll know where the money went.

The following two time-sheets illustrate the legal mind at its creative best:

WHAT THE TIME-SHEET SAYS

CLIENT: Global Magazines plc	
Reviewing active client litigation files	2 hours, 6 minutes
Phone conference with client re same	1 hour
CLIENT: Sarawak Oil Inc.	
Lunch conference with client re outstanding matters, including action being brought by native sheep farmers for environmental damage	2 hours, 18 minutes
CLIENT: Amalgamated Plasterboard Ltd	
Reviewing, editing and revising modified documents	3 hours, 54 minutes
TOTAL BILLABLE TIME	9 hours, 18 minutes

WHAT THE TIME-SHEET *SHOULD* SAY

CLIENT: Global Magazines plc	
Thinking about client's new receptionist during morning job	30 minutes
Reading morning paper	24 minutes
Rummaging through client files for name and number of client's new receptionist	30 minutes
Getting coffee	18 minutes
Getting psyched up to call client's new receptionist re dinner on	
Saturday night, including preparing note to assist re same	1 hour, 18 minutes
Calling client's new receptionist re dinner on Saturday night	12 minutes
CLIENT: Sarawak Oil Inc.	
Three-bottle lunch with client at The River Cottage:	
Discussing client's golf game and recent vacation in St Lucia	1 hour, 42 minutes
Swapping ethnic jokes about Borneo sheep farmers	30 minutes
CLIENT: Amalgamated Plasterboard Ltd	
Proofreading retyped Agreement	1 hour, 18 minutes
Napping at desk	18 minutes
Proofreading re-retyped Agreement	1 hour, 18 minutes
Flirting with sexy trainee	24 minutes
Arranging for copying of re-re-retyped Agreement	42 minutes
TOTAL BILLABLE TIME	9 hours, 18 minutes

Double-Billing

Perhaps the most ingenious device known to the law was conceived in response to the popular misconception that there are only twenty-four hours in a day.

Double-billing, or billing two clients for the same increment of time, occurs most frequently when a lawyer is required to travel. A lawyer based in Leeds who is required to visit London to confer with two clients might bill the four-hour return train trip to each. His rationale is that if he had made the trip for one client alone, he'd have billed that client for all the time – so why not bill all of it to each?

Some lawyers double-bill as a matter of course. None of them, especially not the ones who triple and quadruple bill, acknowledge that it goes on. They're greedy, not stupid.

What they do is bury the double-billed time in the mountain of other items billed to the client in a month or two and no one is the wiser.

The only way clients could monitor this practice would be to have access to what other clients were being billed by the same partner at the same time. They can't do that of course. Confidentiality laws require that lawyers keep their clients' affairs secret.

Confidentiality laws arose about the same time as double-billing.

A TRUE STORY

One day, while crossing the street, a young lawyer was hit by a bus. He died and went to Heaven, where he was cordially greeted by Saint Peter.

'Welcome!' said Saint Peter, 'You must be ready for a rest. Not many people live to be your age.'

'What do you mean?' said the lawyer. 'I'm only 37.'

'Oh no, I'm afraid you're mistaken.' said Saint Peter. 'According to your time-sheets, you're 142 years old.'

CHAPTER 19

LAWYERS IN LOVE

Dealing with romantic
feelings towards a lawyer

Y ou've heard the stories. Everyone has. They're not pretty. Maybe it's happened to someone you know. A friend or colleague. Maybe to someone you love – that's when it really hurts.

What on earth could possess someone to become romantically involved with a lawyer? To anybody who knows the profession, the prospect is about as inviting as falling in love with an old jockstrap. An Italian *unicyclist's* jockstrap, even.

A prominent sociologist once compared the phenomenon of going out with a lawyer to the Cabbage Patch Doll craze that swept the Western world about thirty years ago – except, of course, for the tragic consequences.

6 THINGS TO BRING WITH YOU ON YOUR FIRST DATE WITH A LAWYER
1. Legal pad.
2. Red Bull (industrial strength).

3. Body condom.
4. English–Latin/Latin–English dictionary.
5. iPod.
6. Cash.

And the fact that playing with a Cabbage Patch Doll offers the possibility of sexual gratification. Also, if you go out for dinner, you'll be more popular if you bring a Cabbage Patch Doll. And it's more likely to pick up the bill. In fact going out with a lawyer isn't very much like going out with a Cabbage Patch Doll at all.

Still, some people continue to do it – go out with lawyers, that is.

What is to be done? Sadly, for those already involved, precious little *can* be done. Anyone who has fallen in love with a lawyer is beyond the pale. The only real hope lies in prevention. This can best be accomplished by having nothing to do with lawyers except when it's absolutely necessary, like when you're about to hauled off to jail. Even then you might want to think about it ... you know ... taste the food, have a chat with your prospective cell mate – give it a chance.

For most people, avoiding lawyers comes as naturally as breathing or, perhaps more appropriately, squashing a cockroach. You see a lawyer and think, *there but for the grace of God go I.* You feel the same mixture of pity and revulsion you feel for a drunk in the gutter – except the drunk might be pleasant company.

As difficult as it may be for most people to conceive of falling in love with a lawyer, a few seem to do it every year. What kind of perverse love are we talking about? It's difficult to describe, but if you've ever talked to a sailor who's been away at sea for ten or twelve months, you have an idea of the desperation involved.

It's similar to the craving that pupils at single-sex boarding schools experience towards the end of each term, and which the Governors relieve by bussing in the 1st XV of the nearest boy's school.

Consider the case of Jennifer X. ('X' is not her real name.) We'll call her Jennifer. She was an attractive young woman living in Fulham, SW6. She didn't get asked out very often, though. This is because she actually wasn't *that* attractive. (More than a few people who met her later commented 'I didn't know Wayne Rooney was a transvestite'.) She wasn't all that young, either. But she did live in Fulham.

Jennifer was an unemployed former stockbroker in the City. The economic turmoil of the banking crisis had cost many stockbrokers their jobs. Jennifer was laid off a little while before the turmoil began, admittedly, but that's another story. Inevitably, she had lots of time on her hands, which she used not only to indulge her fondness for Fortnum & Mason truffles, but also to hang around the White Horse on Friday nights in the hope of meeting Mr Right.

Enter Andrew Greenly (his real name; so what if a lawyer is publicly humiliated?). He was a conscientious if modestly talented associate at a large corporate firm in the City, and equipped with about the same social appeal as Jennifer.

Andrew and Jennifer first met on a Club Med holiday in Tunisia. They were both fighting for space at the hors d'oeuvre table, hurling food of every sort in the general direction of their heads.

Perhaps by fate they simultaneously made a grab for the same hors d'oeuvre – the last one of those mini-sausages soaked in honey – and their hands touched. Although both were initially repulsed, their long-starved sexual appetites quickly took over, and they left hand in hand – which repulsed everyone else – but Andrew and Jennifer were past caring about that.

Their immediate infatuation yielded to passion. They spent every night together for the rest of the holiday and the following month. So inflamed was Jennifer's ardour that she was even willing to overlook Andrew's insistence on wearing his suit to bed. 'I think it's the braces,' Andrew would say. 'They make me feel so masterful.'

By the end of the month they were engaged.

Jennifer's enchantment soon turned to frustration. As time went on, Andrew began dragging himself home later and later. It reached the point when Jennifer wouldn't know whether he was coming home at all, and when he did, usually around midnight, he would fall straight asleep (still wearing his suit, as we mentioned).

For a while, Jennifer suspected that he was seeing another woman – some of his sleep-talking sounded vaguely licentious – terms like 'joinder of parties', 'ejectment' and 'post-trial briefs'. As blind as love is, however, she was able to make a realistic assessment of the chances of another woman becoming interested in Andrew and she put the thought out of her mind.

Abstinence wasn't the worst of Jennifer's problems with Andrew. They didn't seem to communicate any more. Andrew had taken to addressing Jennifer in rude condescending tones, which she knew he had picked up from the way partners at the firm addressed him, and the way everyone at the firm addressed non-paying clients. Rather than simply talking with her, he seemed to be lecturing her, and he had the strange habit of summarising his argument at the outset and reserving three minutes for rebuttal.

Jennifer considered breaking off the engagement. All her friends said her goldfish was better company than Andrew, even though it had been floating at the top of the tank for a month. But it's a hard world for short, podgy, odd-looking, untalented former stockbrokers, and she decided to go through with it.

Only after she had had their first child, and realised how much it was going to be like Andrew – try to imagine a hairless rabbit in pinstripes – did Jennifer appreciate the full measure of her mistake.

Jennifer's story is a sad one, the story of a wasted life. But it need not be your story as well.

Learn the lesson of her misfortune. The only way to handle romantic feelings towards a lawyer is not to have any.

Spotting Lawyers Out on the Town

In a better world, lawyers would never set foot outside their offices. They'd just live there – eating, sleeping, billing. Some City firms have already attained this plateau.

Many lawyers still wander the streets, however, and bumping into one can ruin an otherwise perfectly enjoyable Saturday evening.

You're a friendly person. You enjoy meeting new people. But

you have to draw the line somewhere. Hey, if you wanted to be bored, you'd be back at home watching Midsomer Murders.

Suppose you spot a lawyer near you in a pub or restaurant. What do you do? First, look around for others; they usually hunt in packs.

Then, if it's male, try spilling a drink on his trousers. The prospect of losing the crease will have him running for his Corby press. If it's female, aim for the legs; she'll have a back-up pair of tights in her handbag, but the thought of being down to her last pair will have her out of the door in a flash.

If a lawyer should take the clearly inappropriate step of initiating conversation with you, call the police and have him physically thrown out. Don't worry about hurting his feelings; he's used to this type of treatment. Some lawyers go out in public *looking for* abuse, craving that moment of self-discovery when their foreheads crunch against the pavement and their brogues get scuffed.

What if you're not sure whether the person in question *is* a lawyer? When you're seventeen pints into the evening, you may not be able to tell.

The trouble is that you can't just come right out with it and ask him, because what if he's *not* a lawyer? Then, you've probably got a fight on your hands.

Besides, what are the chances of anyone admitting to that kind of thing, especially when he's out in public trying to 'pass'?

Your best bet is to apply one of the following tests:

- Mention that your father is chairman of Glaxo, and that he is looking for a firm to replace his existing solicitors. Then stare into his face. If his pupils dilate and saliva appears at the corner of his mouth, have him thrown out.
- Assert that legal fees should be subject to review by a panel of lay people. If the vein in his forehead starts to throb, have him thrown out.
- State your support for no-fault insurance legislation. If this triggers an outraged polemic on the right of every citizen to defend an action brought against him, have him thrown out.

CONTRACT
Courtenay Bigguns-Lately (the 'Dater')
and
Sally Forth ('The Datee')

1. Notwithstanding Downton Abbey being a bit of a cliff hanger, or a last-minute pick-up at the Stoat and Fox after work, the Dater and the Datee agree to meet at *Chez Pierre's* at 8.30 p.m. on Friday (hereinafter referred to as The Date) always allowing that the Datee may be no more than 20 (twenty) and no less than 10 (ten) minutes late without incurring penalties under Rider 3(i): Emotional Blackmail.

2. It is hereby understood that The Date shall take place in order that the Dater may discuss a couple of really quite interesting ideas he's got for the litigation meeting on Tuesday on which he'd like some creative input from the Datee. Both parties shall terminate such discussion no later than 3 (three) minutes after the polenta has been served, at which point they shall undertake to determine from each other:
   (i) Whether the Dater is still seeing Susan from Accounts (hereinafter referred to as 'A Bit Tarty If You Ask Me, But Then Some Men Go For The Obvious Type');
   (ii) Whether the Datee really stung that fool Nigel in Commercial for a five-course meal at Nobu, plus entrance to Bouji's;
   (iii) How the Dater recalls the very first time he saw the Datee across the Boardroom during another litigation meeting and even though they didn't speak until the Christmas Eve party, he'd always sort of thought, well, you know, she wasn't like the other girls, she was more, like, sensitive.

3. It is hereby agreed that at no time during the period of this contract; shall the Datee draw attention to the following:
   (i) The Dater's choice of the second cheapest bottle of wine;
   (ii) The Dater's belief that it is only a matter of time before Chris Rea makes it big again;

(iii) The Datee's total lack of interest in whether Arsenal should have played Walcott, despite his injury, that afternoon, whoever Walcott is, or, come to that, Arsenal;

4. In consideration for this and notwithstanding that everybody knows who Walcott is, the Dater agrees:
   (i) Not to eat all the after-dinner mints that come with the bill;
   (ii) Not to cause embarrassment by paying with any credit card that causes the waiter to ask the Dater whether he would mind stepping over to the till for just a second, thus making it clear to everybody in the restaurant that the Dater can't even run to a pizza, let alone and inter alia a good bottle of wine.

5. At the termination of the meal, the Dater agrees to conduct the Datee to her place of residence, *always notwithstanding* that should the Datee insist on travelling the seven miles home alone, on foot, through a derelict housing estate and a freight marshalling yard, the Dater shall take this as fair notice to quit.

6. Always provided that the Datee does not leave the Dater standing on the doorstep (ref. That Fool Nigel, passim) the Datee agrees within 5 (five) minutes of crossing the threshold, to make it plain, by word or by deed, whether she is any of the following:
   (i) Not That Sort of Girl on a first date;
   (ii) Not That Sort of Girl after a dodgy meal and a bottle of house red;
   (iii) Entirely That Sort of Girl, but not with the Dater.

7. Should the clauses above be satisfied it is hereintofore agreed that neither party shall cause the following to be uttered:
   (i) I don't do this with everyone I go out with, you know.
   (ii) I'd like to stay, honestly, but I've got football training first thing. Now where's my other sock?
   (iii) You won't tell anyone in the office about this, will you?
   (iv) Damn I Look, er, I'm terribly sorry, I've never had this problem before.
   (v) Funny, that's not what Susan in Accounts says.

- Declare that you've long considered expanding briefcases and Dictaphones to be emblematic of a truly advanced society. If he nods in agreement, have him thrown out.
- Mention your admiration for people who know how to put Her Majesty's Revenue and Customs in its place. If he smiles, puffs out his chest, and launches into a discussion of offshore tax shelters and generation-skipping trusts, have him thrown out. (You may catch an accountant or two with this trick – no loss.)

If, despite all efforts, a lawyer causes irreparable harm to your night out, don't get mad. Get even!

First, ask him for his business card. Take two or three. You never know when you'll back into someone else's car trying to get out of a tight parking space, and want to leave a note under the wipers.

Second, tell him that just a moment ago – what an amazing coincidence! – you were talking to someone who wants to hire a lawyer. And then give him the number of that old school friend who's been trying to sell you a pensions policy for the last six months.

CHAPTER 20

YOU AND YOUR LAWYER

Finding him; using him; keeping him in his place

Sooner or later it happens to everybody. Your life is going along fine, you're keeping up with your mortgage payments, you've just got a big promotion, your sex life is finally heating up – and suddenly disaster strikes. Your playful Great Dane – good old Chewy – dismembers a small child; you have a few too many beers and on the way home decide to chance a red light, only to notice too late the local Chief Constable's elderly mother stepping off the pavement; your wife finds some pink lace underwear in your glove compartment and doesn't buy your story about how much more comfortable you find them than boxer shorts on hot summer afternoons.

Law books are full of such tales of disaster. What makes them disasters is that when they happen you have to consult a lawyer.

You've hoped against hope that you'd never have to do it. You've never felt comfortable around lawyers. You've never associated them with the good things in life.

But now there's really no choice. Like appendicitis, your legal problem won't just go away. You have to *do* something about it – and you can't do it on your own.

The analogy to appendicitis is instructive: getting rid of your legal problem, like having an organ removed, is painful, costly (your lawyer will perform a walletectomy on you) and will leave you permanently scarred.

But since it has to be done, you want it done properly. You don't want to find yourself doing five years for a minor traffic offence.

Selecting Your Lawyer

So how do you go about the critical task of finding a lawyer? Search the web? Stroll down the High Street and pick the first frosted glass window-front?

One of the difficult things about instructing a lawyer is that you don't necessarily get what you pay for. If you go to a big 'name' firm you'll pay a fortune for the privilege, but the quality of advice and the service you receive may be no better, or even worse, than what's available on the High Street at a fraction of the cost.

Particularly if your case is relatively small beer as far as the big firm is concerned: your lawyer will always have more important files to work on and he'll probably hand your matter to his trainee as suitable material on which to cut his teeth. And make mistakes.

The other truism is that, although a *firm* may have an excellent all-round reputation, you as a client will be relying on an *individual's* ability and experience, not the firm's.

Clients tend to make the rather naive assumption that lawyers at the top firms are all roughly as competent as each other. They wouldn't do so if they thought of firms in the same way as, say, racing stables: the stable that produced Desert Orchid trained many other nags who ended their careers in 400g cylindrical tins at Tesco's.

There's the same uneven distribution of talent in a law firm. The lawyer in charge of your case may only be on the payroll because his name bears a striking resemblance to the one at the head of the firm's notepaper, in which case all the expertise in other quarters of the firm will be totally irrelevant to your position. At least as important as the question of *which firm*, then, is the question of *which individual*.

Go by Recommendation

A recommendation is your best bet. Ask your family friends, or business colleagues.

Don't expect glowing praise for any lawyer. No one has anything really good to say about them. Even your local vicar is likely to describe the lawyers he knows in language more commonly heard from Liverpool stevedores. Work to a lower benchmark, so that if someone describes Lawyer X as 'a miserable old sod who hardly ever returns your calls' you recognise it for the high praise it is.

Shop Around

Set up appointments with five or six lawyers – as many as you can stomach. Remember that although the one you eventually instruct will probably bill you for the precious time you squandered in that first interview, the several who you don't will have to absorb the loss. (If one of them bills you for £250, feel free to use the invoice for cat litter – it'll never be worth his while to sue you.)

When you arrive for your appointment, remember that you're the master and he's the servant, whatever it feels like. Some find the prospect of dealing with clients so abhorrent that they'll hold a scented hankie to their nose throughout your meeting. If your lawyer turns out to be one of those, remember that there are dozens of other firms you can turn to. Console yourself with the thought that no matter how bad things are, at least *you're* not a lawyer.

Ask the receptionist to let your lawyer know you've arrived. You will then be kept waiting for between fifteen minutes and an hour – long enough to give you a better idea of the meaning of eternity. Just be grateful that you don't have to stand in a queue.

Waiting rooms will vary from practice to practice. Some are so grubby and down-at-heel, you will begin to feel your problem isn't so bad after all. Others are inappropriately and disgustingly opulent. As you sit there waiting to be called, savour the luxury of filthy but thoughtfully spent lucre: the marble floors, the mahogany-panelled lift, the exotic plants. Try not to think about who's paying for them.

Stay Cool

Eventually a secretary will arrive to escort you to the inner sanctum, where you will finally cast your eyes on the curiosity that may become your lawyer. Keep your wits about you at this stage. Take note of various points of manner, like whether he steps forward to shake your hand; whether he asks his secretary to hold any calls, or subjects you to interruptions from his other clients and/or partners and/or friends. These minor elements of behaviour are a reliable indication of the kind of service you can expect in the future.

Above all, do not be intimidated by him. Ask him what kind of success he's had in recent cases; ask him if he can tell you the names of some recent clients who you can contact for a reference. Make him explain the difference between herringbone and tweed. Remember: he's not your lawyer yet.

Discuss the Fee

One matter you should definitely raise in your initial meeting is the question of fees. Lawyers never bring it up on their own. Even when you ask directly, they can be strangely cryptic in response, as if the subject is too crass for discussion.

Don't be taken in by this pose and reject evasive answers. You don't want to discover too late that your lawyer's casual reference to 'my usual rate' means £600 per hour.

Neither should you settle for 'Oh, I think we can work something out that will be mutually satisfactory.' Hey, if you weren't desperate, you wouldn't be paying him anything.

Be prepared to have to work for an answer. He might attempt full-scale diversionary tactics:

'That's a good question, Ms Stephenson, and I'm glad you had the presence of mind to raise it at the outset. Too often, I think, lawyers are so busy striving to advance their clients' interests that they lose sight of these kinds of questions and neglect to establish any true understanding – or what could be called a meeting of minds – as to how it will all turn out in the long run. Why, I recall one case I had down in Bristol...'

When this romp through irrelevance finishes, repeat the question. Do so again and again until you get a straight answer or the cleaning people come in to vacuum and turn off the lights.

You Call the Tune

The basic rule here is: your lawyer works for you, not vice versa. You pay the piper, you call the tune.

Early on in the relationship you will find your lawyer telling you what you can and cannot do. Nip this in the bud. Tell him what you want, and if he can't make it happen, let him know you're prepared to take your business down the road. If he values your business at all (and lawyers nowadays are having to be a lot less choosy about what they value and what they don't) you will be surprised at how quickly he will determine, after a little additional research, that what you want seems to be possible after all.

Monitor your Lawyer's Work

Every single thing your lawyer does for you starts the meter running. It doesn't matter if he's just *thinking* about sending you a copy letter or an update memo. If he's doing anything that so much as reminds him of you, you'll be billed for the time. What can you do to control this horrific state of affairs?

You have to play him at his own game by monitoring and recording in painstaking detail exactly what benefits you're aware of receiving. Phone calls are a good place to start. Get in the habit of noting down the length of each call you have with your lawyer, when it occurred, what was said, and who initiated it. And don't be embarrassed to let him know you're doing just that, as in 'Thanks for the call, John. I think we covered a lot in *just five minutes*.'

Every letter you write should make it blatantly clear that you are keeping an eye on costs and don't intend to be shafted.

There's nothing at all wrong in saying:

'I enclose the information you requested. *In order to minimise the work your firm will have to do on the case, and hence minimise your costs*, I have filed the documents in chronological order, and highlighted the important points.'

It might aggravate him a little, and he won't like you for it, but when he comes to fill in that all-important time-sheet, he'll err on the side of caution.

If, on the other hand, he gets the idea that you're not too worried about the size of your bill, it will expand in ways you cannot imagine. It will manage to take on expensive dinners, exotic travel and his wife's subscription to *Vogue*, not to mention peripheral research that would have been done anyway for other clients – things that Glaxo may not mind subsidising, but you do.

Keep your Perspective

Try to remember that your lawyer is, after all, only a lawyer. That you go to him to solve a problem, and that you tell him things you would not tell your doctor, best friend or spouse, does not alter the fact that his interest in you is purely commercial.

Your lawyer may sound personally interested in hearing the details of your botched hip operation. You might appreciate his expression of outrage as you describe your wife's infidelities or your husband's violent tendencies when he reaches his sixth scotch of the evening. But remember that each word you utter, your lawyer's meter is clicking away.

If that meter isn't running, your lawyer isn't listening.

DOCTORS V. LAWYERS

Doctors and lawyers are notoriously unfriendly to each other. This seems strange at first, because they're all from the same sort of background, they live in the same streets, they're flip sides of the same professional coin.

Nevertheless, they don't like each other. What eats lawyers is the superior respect enjoyed by the medical profession. Doctors get special parking permits, allowing them to park in places normally reserved for people with no legs. Doctors get to be called 'Doctor', whereas lawyers are plain 'Mr' even at the pinnacle of their profession. Someone who comes bottom of his class at medical school is still called Doctor, whereas someone at the bottom of his class at law school is called 'Waiter!'

And whereas doctors are credited with performing a skilful and valuable social service, lawyers are regarded as bloated leeches feeding on society's misfortunes.

Finally, whereas medical school is still very difficult to get into, practically anybody could get into law school somewhere. Just think about the lawyers you've met. Some are bright enough, but how many will be picking up prizes in Stockholm?

CHAPTER 21

LIFE BEYOND LAW

*What do you mean, I'm not
qualified to do anything else?*

Plenty of people go to law school telling themselves they won't actually practice law; they just want the law degree as a stepping stone toward something more … suitable. They confidently anticipate a life more interesting, more consequential and certainly more elegant than the nail-dirtying Gallipoli-trenches of private law practice.

They see law school as a credential, more than a lark but nothing life-shaping. It's expensive, which reduces its larkfulness, but if it weren't, anybody could do it and then what's the point? No, for these people law school is just a credential, an entrée. It's something nice to have but far from essential – like a doorman.

Get real. When you get out of law school, you'll have (a) huge debts, (b) a far better chance of paying your rent through some form of legal work than through waiting tables (although the latter would be more fun, not to mention more socially useful) and (c) no better idea of what to do with your life than when you graduated from college.

True, if your trust fund is paying for your room, board and tuition, then it really is a lark, so why not? Actually, there are plenty of why-nots, but even law school beats working, because working invariably entails, well, work. But the odds are overwhelming that if you go to law school, you'll end up practising law. Statistics show – okay, statistics don't show squat. Still, over 90 per cent of the people who graduate from law school end up practising law.

Bottom line: going to law school isn't a way to postpone a decision on what to do with your life. Going to law school *is* a decision on what to do with your life. It's a decision to practise law.

TOP 10 THINGS YOU CAN DO WITH YOUR LAW DEGREE OTHER THAN PRACTISE LAW:

1. *Teach* law.
2. Drive a cab.
3. Write lawyer shows on TV.
4. Dig ditches.
5. Become a corrupt, heartless, egocentric, bottom-feeding, social parasite, i.e. run for a seat in Parliament.
6. Go into investment banking and make a fortune through your refined analytical abilities, well-developed negotiating skills, and sophisticated understanding of the twists and turns of the law.

7. Go into investment banking and make a fortune by swapping inside information with your law school class-mates at other investment banks.

8. Marry someone who's (a) impressed by your law degree and (b) rich.

9. Beg your old law firm to take you back.

10. Become a writer, producing books of dubious quality (like this one).

11. Starve.

(Note that this list does not have more than 10 items. Items 10 and 11 are the same.)

CHAPTER 22

LEGAL GLOSSARY

Of foreign and forked tongues

Accord and Satisfaction – 1. The resolution of a claim for breach of contract, whereby the parties agree to alter the original terms. 2. Carnal activity in the back seat of a Honda.

Action – Court case. A term used by lawyers to distract the client from the fact that absolutely nothing is happening on his case.

Adultery – The crime of having more fun than society considers it seemly for an adult to have.

Affidavit – A client's sworn statement of whatever facts his lawyer considers necessary to win the case.

A Fortiori – 'For a still stronger reason.' A Latin term used by lawyers to link an unarguable premise to an inexplicable conclusion.

Allegation – A supposedly factual statement pertaining to proceedings. *See* allegory, fable.

Amicus Curiae – (Latin) 'Friend of the Curious.' The person who works on the Enquiry Desk at the Royal Courts of Justice.

Arbitrator – Independent Negotiator. Derived from a combination of *arbitrary* and *traitor*.

Arguendo – (Latin) 'For the sake of argument.' Hypothetically speaking. Not to be confused with *innuendo* – A popular Italian suppository.

Bankruptcy – Life after debt.

Brief – A legal term which, to the extent that it suggests brevity, constitutes the only one-word oxymoron in the English language.

Briefcase – A leather lunch box.

Capital Gains Tax – Accrual and unusual punishment.

Contributory Negligence – In London, the doctrine that anyone who leaves their car guarded by anything less than a squad of SAS is as much to blame as the person who stole it.

Damnun Absque Injuria – (Latin) 'Loss without injury.' A polite reference to the retirement of non-productive senior partners. *See* Rule against Perpetuities; Deadwood.

Deadwood – Anyone in your firm senior to you.

Dictaphone – A battery-powered device beloved by lawyers for its inability to fall asleep during legal monologues.

Euthanasia – A system of early retirement often urged on highly paid senior lawyers by their younger partners.

Ex Lax – (Latin) 'From the lawyer.' Refers to memos, briefs and other work product of lawyers.

Fee Tail – A restricted form of property ownership. Not to be confused with 'Free Tail' (*see* Club 18–30).

Force Majeure – An irresistible force that prevents you from fulfilling your contractual obligations; such as a storm, flood, war or the realisation that you could make a much bigger profit elsewhere.

Habeas Corpus – (Latin) 'You've got a body.' A chat-up line used at legal conventions.

Hung Jury – A divided jury. Ironic term, because if the jury's hung, the defendant isn't.

Layman – What lawyers call the person they screw.

Legal Pad – 1. The residence of a cool lawyer. 2. That extra something built into a lawyer's bill.

Litigation – A basic right of the legal system, which guarantees every aggrieved person his decade in court.

Nuisance – Wrongful interference with someone's use and enjoyment of his property; for example, your thoughtless upstairs neighbour who insists on playing loud hip hop at times when decent people like you are trying to sleep – not to mention the rude insomniac downstairs who has taken to banging on his ceiling with a broom handle just because he can't appreciate the tasteful melodies (and other rhythmic sounds) that emanate from your flat at various reasonable times.

Objection – The strangulated cry of a lawyer who sees truth about to enter the courtroom (USA only).

Paralegal – A legal secretary who can't type.

Parole – A conditional release from prison, usually allowing the convict to demonstrate the inadequacy of the original sentence.

Rainmaker – A lawyer whose compensation bears no relation to his legal skills.

Res Ipsa Loquitur – (Latin) 'The thing speaks for itself.' A legal defence to the crime of killing mother-in-laws.

Settlement – A device by which lawyers obtain fees without working for them.

Tax Lawyer – Someone with a flair for numbers but without the personality to be an accountant.

Usufruct – 1. In real property law, the right to enjoy the fruits of land owned by someone else. 2. An Italian gesture of contempt.

Vagina – Aren't you a little old to be looking up words like this?

Will – A device that lets you wait until you're out of harm's way before revealing how you really felt about your spouse and children.